D1065842

Getting a Grip on the Basics

Building a Firm Foundation
for the Victorious Christian Life

by
Beth A. Jones

Harrison House
Tulsa, Oklahoma

Unless otherwise indicated, all Scripture quotations are taken from the *King James Version* of the Bible.

Scripture quotations marked AMP are taken from *The Amplified Bible*. *Old Testament* copyright © 1965, 1987 by the Zondervan Corporation. *New Testament* copyright © 1958, 1987 by The Lockman Foundation. Used by permission.

15 14 13 12   38 37 36 35 34 33

Getting a Grip on the Basics:
Building a Firm Foundation
For the Victorious Christian Life
ISBN-13: 978-1-57794-826-1
ISBN-10: 1-57794-826-2
(formerly ISBN 0-89274-625-4)
Copyright © 1994 by Beth Ann Jones
P.O. Box 555
Richland, Michigan 49083

Published by Harrison House, Inc.
P.O. Box 35035
Tulsa, Oklahoma, 74153

Printed in the United States of America.
All rights reserved under International Copyright Law.
Contents and/or cover may not be reproduced in whole or in part in any form without the expressed written consent of the Publisher.

On this date, _____,

I received Jesus Christ
as my Savior and Lord

at _____.

_____
(your signature)

The following people
were witnesses to my new birth:

_____

_____

Contents

Acknowledgments

I am deeply indebted to many people who took time to teach me the basics!

I would like to honor those whom the Lord used: from my childhood friend and college roommate, Andrea Hammack who led me to the Lord, to the various Bible study leaders that poured into my life, to the Campus Crusade for Christ staff at Western Michigan University and Boston University, to Pastor Dave Williams and Mount Hope Church in Lansing, Michigan, to the faculty at Rhema Bible Training Center in Broken Arrow, Oklahoma and to many others the Lord used along the way; I honor you and I thank you for planting the seed of the Word into my heart.

For over 15 years, we have seen the Lord use this book to help establish those who are new or young in Christ and refresh those who are mature in the Lord. Today, Getting a Grip on the Basics has been translated into over a dozen foreign languages and is being used around the world. The free PDF download of those translations are available at www.gettingagriponthebasics.com.

We pray the Lord continues to pour out His grace on each page – in this English version and in every foreign translation - and may many more people be rooted and grounded in Christ through their study in Get a Grip. May much eternal fruit - in and through the lives of those who study these pages – be produced for His glory and His kingdom purposes.

Him we preach, warning every man and teaching every man in all wisdom,
that we may present every man perfect in Christ Jesus. To this end I also labor,
striving according to His working which works in me mightily.

Colossians 1:28-29, NKJV

Introduction

After the birth of our first child, our pediatrician told us three essential things we needed to provide for our newborn. They were love, nourishment and protection. These same three elements are necessary for every newborn Christian, as well. That is the reason we have written this workbook. Through studying the Scriptures and completing this workbook, you will find and experience the love of God, you will receive spiritual nourishment and you will be able to rest in the protective care of the Lord and His Word.

Every believer needs to be grounded in the fundamentals of the Word of God. This workbook will be helpful to new Christians, as well as to mature Christians who want to be renewed in the basics of their faith.

We have written the lessons so that they can be completed by just one person who wants to work at his or her own pace or by a group of people who want to study together. At the end of each lesson there is both a Personal Application and a Group Exercise section to accommodate both types of study.

> **...Christ in you, the hope of glory: whom we preach, warning every man, and teaching every man in all wisdom; that we may present every man perfect in Christ Jesus.**
>
> **Colossians 1:27,28**

GUIDELINES FOR STUDY

A. GUIDELINES FOR INDIVIDUAL STUDY

1. Set aside a regular time each week when you can get alone with God and study the lessons in this workbook.

2. Pray and ask the Lord to illuminate His Word to you each time you study.

3. Look up each Scripture and take time to think upon the Word of God.

4. Don't be in a hurry to complete the workbook; rather, move through the book at a steady pace and allow the Holy Spirit to minister to you personally.

B. GUIDELINES FOR GROUP STUDY

1. A group can consist of two or more people. It is important to have one leader, preferably a mature Christian, who can facilitate the group study and discussion.

2. Determine a regular time and a quiet location for the group to meet together to study the lessons in this workbook each week.

3. Pray and ask the Lord to illuminate His Word each week.

4. Look up the Scriptures and take turns reading them aloud.

5. Make each person in the group feel welcome and important; encourage each one to participate. Do not allow one person to dominate all the discussion.

6. Take time to allow for group discussion and interaction during the lessons, but avoid getting off track with side issues.

7. Don't be in a hurry to complete the workbook; rather, maintain a steady progression through the lessons and allow the Holy Spirit the freedom to minister to each individual in the group.

8. It is wise to assign the next lesson as homework each week. After the group members have done their individual study, they will be more familiar with the material. Encourage group members to write down any questions they might have and present them for discussion the next time you meet together.

When it comes to eternal considerations, nothing matters more than making sure you qualify for eternal life in heaven. What are the qualifications?

CHAPTER ONE

HOW TO BECOME A CHRISTIAN

A. THE BIG QUESTION

How do you know if you are a Christian? What must you do to be saved? Does going to church or being a good person make you a Christian or guarantee you eternal life? Does it really matter what you believe? These are all questions of eternal importance.

When it comes to eternal considerations, nothing matters more than making sure you qualify for eternal life in heaven. What are the qualifications?

B. THE QUALIFICATIONS FOR ETERNAL LIFE

1 John 5:11-13

Who grants eternal life?_____

Where is it found? _____

Who has eternal life? _____

Who doesn't have eternal life? _____

A person who believes in Jesus Christ, the Son of God, can _____ *(choose correct word)* that he has eternal life.

☐ Hope   ☐ guess   ☐ wish
☐ feel   ☐ know   ☐ pray

ETERNAL LIFE: Eternal life is not only a quantity of life, or a span of timelessness in which to live, but also it is a quality of life that includes abundance. It is the God-kind of life that Jesus lived.

C. HOW DO YOU KNOW YOU HAVE ETERNAL LIFE?

Do you *know* for sure that you have eternal life?

1. Yes, I know that I have eternal life. _____

   How do you know? _____

   _____

2. No, I am not sure I have eternal life._____

If you are not sure you have eternal life, or if you have questions you would like to have answered, then the study in Scripture that follows will clarify that *knowing* for you.

D. WHO IS JESUS?

Christianity revolves around one central Person: Jesus Christ. Jesus is the most unique Person in history. He claimed to be God! This claim puts Jesus in a different league than any other religious leader in history.

1. Jesus claimed to be God.

Was Jesus Christ truly God? Was His birth, life, ministry, death and resurrection proof of His claim that He was God manifested in the flesh?

a. What did Jesus say about Himself?

John 4:25,26 _____

John 10:30_____

John 14:8,9 _____

b. What did others say about Jesus?

John 1:1,14 (John) _____

John 20:25-28 (Thomas) _____

John 5:18; 10:33 (Jews) _____

Colossians 1:15-18 (Paul)_____

c. What do you say about Jesus?

_____ I believe He is God.

_____ I am not sure what I believe at this time.

I believe _____

_____

_____

2. Jesus came for a purpose.

John 10:10

Why did Jesus come to this earth? _____

_____

In your own words, describe abundant life as you understand it _____

_____

Who is the thief? _____

Why did he come? _____

Are you experiencing abundant life, or are you experiencing a lifestyle lacking in meaning, joy and purpose?_____

Describe your life. _____

_____

_____

_____

3. Jesus rose from the dead.

1 Corinthians 15:3-6

What did Jesus do that no other person has done? _____

_____

How many people saw Jesus after His resurrection?_____

If Jesus truly rose from the dead, as the Scriptures say, then He is still alive. How does His resurrection affect our faith in Jesus today?_____

E. WHO ARE WE?

We have looked at Who Jesus is. Now let's look at who we are. Do we really need Jesus? Why do we need a Savior? What is our condition apart from God?

1. Is everyone a sinner?

SIN: To sin means "to miss the mark."[1] We could understand sin in terms of archery — that is, to sin means to miss the bull's eye. When an arrow hits any of the rings outside the bull's eye, it has missed the mark. In the same way, our fallen human nature (which we inherited from Adam, the father of the human race) has caused us to miss the bull's eye of God's perfection. We have missed the mark of God's glory. The fallen human nature is a sin nature (a nature that misses the mark).

   a. Romans 3:23

   Who has sinned? _____

There is a difference between our sin nature and our sinful acts. Sinful acts are the *result* of our sin nature. It is the sin nature that God is primarily concerned with. This inherited sin nature separates us from God. If God can change the sin nature in us, then our desire to commit sinful acts will also change.

   b. Romans 5:12

   To whom has death come? _____

DEATH: Three types of death are described in the Bible: spiritual death, physical death and the second death (also called eternal death). If a person is not born again, his spirit (or heart), the part of him that contacts God, is separated from God — he is spiritually dead. Spiritual death is not cessation of being; rather, it is a separation from God. Physical death occurs when life departs from the physical body. The second death will occur after the Great White Throne of Judgment when everyone who has not received the Lord Jesus Christ (whose names are not found written in the Lamb's Book of Life) will be cast into the lake of fire, eternally separated from God. (See Revelation 20:11-15.)

2. Where did sin come from?

   a. 1 John 3:8

   Who has sinned from the beginning? _____

   What does this say about those who sin?_____

   _____

   b. John 8:44

   Who does Jesus say is the father of these religious leaders (unbelievers)? _____

   In what way did they imitate their father? _____

   _____

We can see from the Scriptures that Satan is the father of all sin and the father of all those who reject Jesus as their Lord.

3. What are the results of sin?

   a. Isaiah 59:2

   What is the result of sin? _____

   b. Romans 6:23

   What are the wages of sin? _____

4. What is our condition apart from God?

   a. Ephesians 2:1-3

   What is our condition before we meet Christ? _____

   _____

   _____

   When we walk according to the course of this world, whose influence are we under?

   _____

   How many of us lived in this condition? _____

   b. Mark 7:21-23

   What is the condition of our heart without Christ? _____

   c. Matthew 23:27

   How does this verse describe those who act religious but who still have an ungodly,

   unbelieving heart? _____

   d. Ezekiel 36:26,27

   What did God promise He would do to solve the problem of man's heart? _____

   _____

Mankind is in a dilemma. First, we see that Jesus came to give us an abundant life; but, because of the fall of man, we have a sin nature and have become separated from God. We have lost our access to the abundant life. Sin has separated us from God and from the abundant life Jesus promised. What did Jesus do to solve the sin problem?

F. JESUS DIED FOR PEOPLE LIKE US

Jesus died for people just like you and me. We might look clean and polished on the outside, but apart from Christ we are void of true life. Sin has been the problem of man's heart since the Garden of Eden, but Jesus came to solve the sin problem once and for all. Jesus came to give us a new heart (or spirit); but in order to do so, He had to give His life. Jesus hung upon a cross and gave His life so that we could have eternal life.

1. 1 Peter 3:18

   Why did Christ suffer and die? _____

   For what purpose? _____

2. Hebrews 9:22

   Under the Old Covenant, the Israelites were required to sacrifice a spotless lamb and shed its blood to atone for (to cover) their sin. If they neglected to do this, their sin was held against them. In the New Covenant, Jesus came as the spotless Lamb of God to shed His blood once and for all to forgive the sin of all mankind.

   If Jesus hadn't died and shed His blood, what would have happened to our sin? _____

   _____

3. Romans 5:8

   For whom did Jesus die? _____

   _____

G. JESUS WILL GIVE US A NEW LIFE

1. 2 Corinthians 5:17

   What happens to a person who is in Christ? _____

   What happens to a person's old life? _____

   _____

2. John 3:1-6

Jesus told Nicodemus that a person cannot enter the kingdom of God unless he is what? *(vv. 3,5.)* _____

_____

BORN AGAIN: Being born again is also called the "new birth." When you are born again spiritually, you receive a recreated heart (spirit) from God; that is, your heart or spirit is born again and is now in contact or in relationship with God. Another way to explain this is that when your spirit or heart is born again, God gives you a new nature.

This new heart (or spirit) gives you a new nature and brings you into a father/child relationship with God. You are actually transferred, or adopted, into the family of God. You become a child of God and a member of His family through the new birth. A preacher once said that it isn't important what *church* you belong to, it's important which *family* you belong to.

3. John 1:12

How does a person become born again and become a child of God? _____

_____

4. Colossians 1:12,13

What family (kingdom) have we been delivered from through the new birth? _____

_____

What family (kingdom) are we translated into? _____

_____

H. IS JESUS THE ONLY WAY TO GOD?

We have looked at the condition of our heart before God, and we have seen God's provision for cleansing us of our sin through the blood of Jesus and giving us a new nature or heart (or spirit) because of the death and resurrection of the Lord Jesus Christ. Maybe you find yourself thinking, *This seems so straight and narrow. Isn't there any other way to get to God? Isn't there any other way to get eternal life?*

What if a person believes in God but not in Jesus Christ? There are many different beliefs about God, Jesus and eternal life — as you can tell by the multitude of religions. The strongest and most sincere beliefs, however, will not change the facts. What are the facts? Again, we must turn to our source, the Word of God, for the facts. Let's look at the Scriptures and see if there is another route by which we can get to God.

1. Matthew 7:13,14

Describe the way that leads to life (eternal). _____

_____

2. John 14:6

   Did Jesus say He was "**a way**" or "**the way**"? _____

   Who goes to the Father apart from Jesus? _____

3. Acts 4:12

   Is there any other name given whereby we can find salvation? _____

   _____

4. 1 Timothy 2:5

   How many mediators are there between God and man? _____

   Who is the Mediator? _____

5. 1 John 2:22,23

   A person who denies Jesus is the Christ is called what? _____

   Does a person who rejects the Son have the Father? _____

   Is there any way a person can believe in the Father and not believe in the Son? (v. 23.) ___

   _____

6. 1 John 4:15

   In order for God to live in you and for you to live in God, Whom must you confess? ____

   _____

7. Ephesians 2:8,9

   What about religion and good deeds? Man's ego wants to **do** something to be saved. What does this verse call salvation? _____

   Is salvation something we earn by being religious or by doing good works? _____

   Can we take any credit for obtaining salvation? _____

SALVATION: This is the all-inclusive word of the gospel! The use of this word in the Bible includes forgiveness of sins; deliverance from danger, captivity, and judgment; health and healing of the body; help, welfare, safety, victory, freedom from prison, preservation of life and physical health; final and complete deliverance from all the curse, including death.[2] Salvation is a free gift. Gifts are not earned, they are simply received.

Jesus won't force Himself on you, but you can receive Him, if you will. God has provided the one and only answer for the problem of man's heart condition (or fallen nature), and that answer is Jesus. Jesus Christ is God's only provision for our sin. It is up to us to believe on and receive Him.

I. WHAT DOES IT MEAN TO BELIEVE AND RECEIVE?

1. John 3:16

   Who can believe in Jesus? _____

   What are the results of believing? _____

   _____

   Becoming a Christian involves **believing** on the name of Jesus and **receiving** Jesus Christ as Lord.

2. Romans 10:9

   What are we to confess with our mouth? _____

   _____

   What are we to believe in our heart? _____

   _____

   What are the results? _____

   _____

CONFESS: We receive salvation by a combination of what we say with our mouth and what we believe in our heart. "To confess" means to acknowledge, to agree with and to say the same thing as. To confess our belief in Jesus as Lord means to acknowledge, and to agree and to say that Jesus is Lord.

To say that Jesus is Lord is to say that He is **your** Lord. Think about what that means. It is not something to be taken lightly or just spoken casually. When you take Jesus as your Lord, you are giving Him control of your life. You are turning the steering wheel of your life over to Him. You are putting yourself in a position of submission to His leadership.

Certainly Jesus is capable of directing your life much better than you are. Since He knows your future, in detail, He can direct your paths into what is best for you. Although Jesus is the Lord of all creation, He gives you the opportunity to exercise your free will and to make Him your personal Lord.

3. John 12:42,43

What does God say about those who don't confess Jesus as Savior? _____

_____

4. Matthew 10:32,33

What does Jesus promise if you confess Him before others? _____

_____

J. PERSONAL APPLICATION

How do I become a Christian?

After looking at the qualifications for eternal life, you may be asking the question, "How do I become a Christian?" Becoming a Christian is the most important decision you will ever make. Your eternal destiny depends upon your decision to accept or reject Jesus Christ. Receiving Jesus Christ into your life will guarantee your eternal destiny — a home in heaven.

Your decision to believe and receive the Lord Jesus Christ involves your total being — spirit, soul and body. When you receive Christ, you are inviting Him to be the Lord of your life, to cleanse you from all sin and to make you a new creature in Christ. When you invite Jesus into your life, you will begin to experience what He has created you for, all along. That God-shaped vacuum and void inside of you will be filled at last.

Just knowing about Christ intellectually or just having an emotional feeling about Jesus is not enough. Receiving Jesus requires an act of your will. In other words, by faith you choose to invite Jesus Christ into your life to be your Lord.

When you confess Jesus with your mouth and believe in your heart that God raised Him from the dead, He will instantly enter your life and cause your spirit to be born again.

1. Do you believe that Jesus is Lord?_____

2. Do you believe God raised Him from the dead? _____

3. Would you like to invite Jesus Christ into your life to be your Lord and Savior?_____

_____

If your answer to these three questions is yes, then make certain of your eternal destiny now by receiving Jesus Christ into your heart and into your life. To ask Jesus Christ to be your Savior, pray a simple prayer, like the one below, and mean it in your heart.

Dear God, I come to You in the name of Jesus. I need You. I know that I am a sinner in need of a Savior. I now turn to You, Jesus. I believe that You died for me and were raised from the dead by God. I believe that You are the Lord, and I now confess You as my Lord. Thank You that I am now born again. I am saved and am a part of Your family. Thank You, Lord.

K. GROUP EXERCISE

There may be people in the group who have questions. Take time to answer any questions those in your group might have.

Read through the Personal Application section as a group. Then, as a group, pray with those who desire to receive Jesus Christ as their Lord.

---

[1]James Strong, *The Exhaustive Concordance Compact Edition with Dictionaries of Hebrew & Greek Words* (Grand Rapids: Baker Book House, 1992), "Greek Dictionary of the New Testament," p.10, #264, #266. Information contained in this explanation of sin is also based on Finis Jennings Dake, *Dake's Annotated Reference Bible* (Lawrenceville, Georgia: Dake Bible Sales, 1961), "New Testament," p. 93, ref. v, column 4, and *Wuest Word Studies in Greek New Testament* (Grand Rapids: Eerdman's Publishing Co., 1945), vol. 3, p. 95.

[2]Finis Jennings Dake, *Dake's Annotated Reference Bible*, (Lawrenceville, Georgia: Dake Bible Sales, 1961), pp. 126,174, s.v. "salvation."

CHAPTER TWO

HOW TO BE SURE YOU ARE A CHRISTIAN

A. WE BASE OUR FAITH ON FACTS

You may ask, "What if I have doubts whether or not I am born again?"

The enemy's first tactic is to cast doubt on the work God has done in your heart. He will try to plant thoughts in your mind to convince you that you are not really born again. One day you may really think you are saved and the next day you may not; therefore, you can see that your intellect is not a good judge to go by. The enemy may also try to make you feel as if you are not saved. One day you may feel very born again and the next day you may not. Therefore, your feelings or any emotional experiences you may have are not a good standard to go by.

How do you know that you are truly a born-again Christian? How do you know you have eternal life? How do you counterattack the enemy when he works against your mind and feelings? The first thing you need to know is that your assurance of salvation is based on the authority of God's Word, not on your intellect or emotional feelings.

You must go by the facts. Facts do not change. What are the facts? God's Word contains the unchanging facts. God's Word is the only source of stability concerning your Christian life. God knows every fact; His Word contains the facts. Faith is our trust in God and His Word. Feelings are the *result* of our faith. We do not depend on feelings or emotions to be saved; we are saved by placing our trust in God.

B. TAKE THE ASSURANCE TEST

1. Facts

   Do Bible facts ever change? _____

2. Feelings

   Do our feelings ever change? _____

   What determines our feelings?_____

3. Faith

   What happens if our faith is in our feelings?_____

   _____

What happens if our faith is in the fact of God's Word? _____

_____

C. WHAT ARE THE FACTS?

What are the facts? God's Word is fact. According to the Bible, what can you be assured of now that you have believed on and received Jesus Christ as your Savior?

1. 1 John 5:11-13

   How do you know you have eternal life? _____

   _____

2. Revelation 3:20

   How do you know Christ came into your life? _____

   _____

3. John 1:12

   How do you know you became a child of God? _____

   _____

4. Colossians 1:14

   What do you know you've received for your sins? _____

   _____

5. John 6:37

   How do you know Jesus Christ has received you? _____

   _____

6. 2 Corinthians 5:17

   What have you become in Christ? _____

   _____

   What has happened to the old you? _____

   _____

7. Romans 8:16

How do you know that you are a child of God?_____

_____

8. 1 John 4:7

How do you know that you are born of God and know God? _____

_____

9. Hebrews 13:5

What do you know that Jesus Christ will never do? _____

_____

Facts, faith and feelings: A preacher once expressed this idea of believing the facts of God's Word when he said, "God said it. I believe it. And that settles it!"

D. PERSONAL APPLICATION

1. Are you sure you are a Christian? _____

On what authority do you base your assurance? _____

_____

2. On the inside cover of your Bible (or somewhere you can keep a permanent record) write down the date and time you received Jesus. You may have to estimate. Whenever the enemy tries to confuse you with doubts about your salvation, just tell him the date and time you received Jesus Christ as your Lord and Savior. Also, in the future, you will appreciate having a record of this very important date.

3. Begin to grow in your new life with Christ.

Take time each day to get to know Him. Commit yourself to studying the Word of God and the lessons that follow in this series, and you will see your relationship with the Lord grow and develop.

E. GROUP EXERCISE

Each person in the group take three minutes and share with the others your story of receiving Christ as your Savior and Lord.

For example:

One minute — My life before I met Christ

One minute — How I met Christ

One minute — My life after receiving Christ

Sharing your testimony and hearing the testimony of others are exciting experiences in the Christian life. Make it a habit to share your testimony with others as a witness of what Christ has done for you.

CHAPTER THREE

HOW TO DEVELOP YOUR RELATIONSHIP WITH GOD

A. WHAT IS GOD LIKE?

Becoming a Christian is the beginning of developing a relationship with God. God is a person — not a force, or a vapor, or an invisible eye. He wants to talk to you, and He wants you to talk to Him. When you meet new friends, it takes many hours of communicating to really get to know them. God has become your friend, and He is the most interesting and loving person you will ever know. Jesus said, **This is life eternal, that they might know thee the only true God, and Jesus Christ, whom thou hast sent** (John 17:3).

The deep cry of every person's heart is to know God. Each person has a built-in spiritual craving to know his Creator. This hunger can only be satisfied by spending time getting to know Him. The primary way to receive spiritual fulfillment and to grow in your relationship with God is to establish a daily quiet time of prayer and Bible reading.

What is your new friend like? He has revealed Himself in His Word, the Bible. How do the following verses describe God?

1. Who is God?

   Matthew 28:19

   God is one God, revealed in three persons. What three persons make up the Godhead?

   a. _____

   b. _____

   c. _____

2. What do these Scriptures tell us about God the Father?

   a. Matthew 7:11 _____

   b. John 4:23,24 _____

   _____

   c. Hebrews 12:9 _____

   _____

d. James 1:17 _____

In your own words, describe the qualities of a good father _____

_____

_____

3. What do these Scriptures tell us about Jesus, the Son?

a. John 8:12 _____

b. John 10:14 _____

c. Hebrews 13:8 _____

d. Galatians 3:13 _____

JESUS, OUR REDEEMER: Jesus Christ has redeemed us from the curse of the Law. The term "the Law" usually refers to the Pentateuch, the first five books of the Bible. According to these five books, we can see that the curse of the Law, or the result of breaking God's law is threefold: poverty, sickness and eternal death. Jesus, through His death, burial and resurrection, redeemed us from this curse. In other words, He freed us from the bondage of poverty, the destruction of sickness and disease and the eternal separation from God. All we have to do is believe and have faith in Him as our Redeemer.

4. What do these Scriptures tell us about the Holy Spirit?

a. 1 Corinthians 3:16 _____

b. John 16:13,14 _____

c. Romans 8:14 _____

d. Romans 8:16 _____

B. HOW DO I GET TO KNOW GOD?

1. Do what Enoch did

Enoch was a man who knew God. He is only mentioned a few times in the Bible, but his example is one each of us can follow. His name means dedicated.[1] Enoch was dedicated to God.

Let's look at the Scriptures to see what Enoch did to get to know God.

a. Genesis 5:24

What did Enoch do? _____

Describe what it means to walk with or fellowship closely with someone who is a friend.

_____

_____

b. Hebrews 11:5

What did God think about Enoch? _____

_____

2. Put God first

We can live a life pleasing to God, just like Enoch did, by doing what Enoch did. Enoch put God first. Every day we have decisions to make and responsibilities to take care of. Each day, whether we realize it or not, we take care of those duties that are a priority to us. Where should God fit in our daily priorities?

a. Matthew 6:33

What does God say we should seek first? _____

_____

What is the result of putting God first? _____

_____

b. Colossians 3:1,2

What things are we to seek, now that we are Christians?_____

_____

What do you think Paul means by seeking "those things that are above"?_____

_____

c. Luke 10:38-42

What was it about Mary that Jesus commended? _____

_____

What was it about Martha that we need to be aware of? _____

It is easy to get too busy. What things are taking too much of your time?_____

_____

3. Seek God with your whole heart

   a. Revelation 3:15,16

      What does God think about those believers who are lukewarm, or half-hearted, toward Him?_____

      _____

   b. Psalm 119:2

      How are we to seek God? _____

   c. Jeremiah 29:13

      When will we really get to know God, or find Him?_____

      _____

   d. Matthew 5:6

      We will be filled with God when we do what?_____

      _____

      In your own words, describe what it is like to hunger and thirst for God. _____

      _____

4. What are the results of seeking God?

   a. 2 Chronicles 7:14

      Who is to seek God? _____

      What four things are we to do? _____

      _____

      _____

      What does God promise to do? _____

_____

b. 2 Chronicles 16:9

What type of person are the eyes of the Lord ever seeking for? _____

_____

What does God want to do for that person? _____

_____

c. Psalm 34:10

Those who seek the Lord will not lack what? _____

d. Proverbs 8:17

When we seek God what happens? _____

e. Hebrews 11:6

What does God do for those who diligently seek Him? _____

5. Examples of those who sought God

a. 1 Chronicles 28:9

Solomon was instructed to know God and to serve God. How was he supposed to do this?

_____

b. 2 Chronicles 31:20,21

How did Hezekiah seek his God? _____

What was the result? _____

c. Ezra 7:10

Ezra prepared his heart so he could do what three things? _____

_____

_____

C. PERSONAL APPLICATION

Deuteronomy 30:19,20

Our Christian life is a result of choices we make. God will never force Himself or His will upon us. He has given us a free will to choose life or death, blessings or curses.

Do you choose to seek God first?_____

Getting to know God by seeking Him daily is a lifelong commitment. Just as marriage is a commitment in which two people choose to spend the rest of their lives getting to know one another, so too is our relationship with God.

Getting to know someone takes time. It also takes effort, patience, talking and listening. It takes seeking out the company of one another. It takes your whole heart to really get to know someone well. God wants us to walk with Him, just as we would walk with our spouse or *our best friend.*

What are some specific ways you can begin to put God first and seek Him with all of your heart? _____

_____

_____

_____

Are there any attitudes, habits, or activities in your life that you need to change in order to make God your number one priority? List them: _____

_____

D. GROUP EXERCISE

Take time as a group to share the ways that each of you seeks God. How does each person spend time reading the Bible or praying? Discuss the benefits of the different approaches each person uses.

What differences have you seen in your life when you are seeking God and when you are not?

What type of activities hinder you from seeking God daily?

---

[1]James Strong, *The Exhaustive Concordance of the Bible* (McLean: MacDonald Publishing, 1978), "Hebrew and Chaldee Dictionary," p. 41, #2585, #2596.

CHAPTER FOUR

HOW TO TALK TO GOD

A. HOW DO I TALK TO GOD?

Prayer is simply talking with God from your heart. Prayer is your avenue for communicating with God. You will want to begin a daily habit of talking to the Lord. This is something you must schedule into your day right from the beginning. Also, because prayer is such a vital time for each Christian, this is one area the enemy works especially hard to hinder or destroy. In just a couple of weeks you can develop the habit of daily prayer so that talking to God will become as natural to you as breathing.

Some of your first questions might be, "What is prayer? To Whom do I pray? What do I pray about? Is God interested in every part of my life or just in the major things? How do I know that God really hears me?" Let's look at the Scriptures to see what God says about prayer.

1. Jesus' example of prayer

   What can you learn from Jesus' example in prayer?

   Mark 1:35 _____

2. Attitudes in prayer

   a. Psalm 5:1-3 _____

   b. Psalm 55:17 _____

   c. Psalm 62:8 _____

   d. Psalm 63:1 _____

3. Promises to answer prayer

   God does hear and answer prayer. What has God promised?

   a. Jeremiah 33:3 _____

   b. Matthew 7:7-11 _____

   c. Hebrews 4:16 _____

   d. Ephesians 3:20 _____

4. When should we pray?

    a. 1 Thessalonians 5:17 _____

    b. Philippians 4:6,7 _____

    What should our attitude be when we pray? _____

    _____

5. For whom should we pray?

    a. 1 Timothy 2:1-4 _____

    b. Ephesians 6:18 _____

    c. Matthew 9:36-38 _____

    d. Luke 6:28 _____

When you are first starting your prayer life, it is helpful to make a list of the people you want to pray for. Take a few moments and, based on the above Scriptures, write down the names of people you have on your heart to pray for. _____

_____

_____

_____

6. Conditions to answered prayer

    There are certain conditions to being effective in prayer. What are these conditions?

    a. John 16:23,24

        To Whom do we pray? _____

        In Whose name do we pray? _____

    b. John 15:7 _____

    c. Mark 11:24 _____

    d. 1 John 5:14,15 _____

        How can we know God hears us? _____

If we know God hears us, what can we expect? _____

_____

GOD'S WILL: God's will is already revealed in His Word, the Bible. God's Word and God's will are identical. His will is His Word.

If you are praying about something that is in line with God's Word, you can be confident you are praying according to God's will. If you are praying about something that is not clearly revealed in God's Word, then in order to determine if it is God's will for your life, see if there would be any hindrances to your prayer, as discussed in Section 8 that follows. If there are no hindrances, you can be confident you are praying according to God's will.

7. The role of faith in prayer

What role does faith play in receiving an answer to prayer?

FAITH: Faith begins where the will of God is known. God's will is revealed in His Word. In a nutshell, faith is simply taking God at His Word. Faith is believing and acting like what God has said in His Word is true! Your faith can grow as you hear the Word of God.

Let's look at the workings of faith.

a. Faith and patience

God hears your prayer the first time you pray. God sends the answer the first time you pray. However, we have an enemy, Satan, who is the god of this world, and he will do whatever he can to hinder us from receiving the answers to our prayers. It is at this point that we have to exercise our faith with patience. We have to maintain our belief in the promises of God. We must walk by faith and not by sight. As we stay in faith, refusing to doubt, the answer God sent to us will be manifested.

Hebrews 10:35,36 _____

Hebrews 6:12,15 _____

James 1:3,4 _____

_____

b. Faith and confession

What we say, or confess, is vital to successful prayer. People who say negative things all the time will rarely receive consistent answers to their prayers because their negative confession negates their faith. God is a God of faith, and faith is positive, not negative.

CONFESSION: Confession means to say the same thing as. A "confession of sin" is to say the same thing about sin as God says. A "confession of faith" is to say the same thing about faith or anything God has to say about us in His Word. It is verbally agreeing with God. Your words can be a key to unlock the door to answered prayer.

Hebrews 10:23

What does this verse teach us about our confession of faith? _____

_____

_____

Mark 11:23

Jesus emphasized the importance of what we say in this verse. How many times did Jesus use the word "say" in this verse? _____

How many times did Jesus use the word "believe"? _____

The words of our mouth are very important. It is a good practice to put a guard on your mouth. Make it a point to discipline yourself to say only those things you believe are in accordance with God's Word.

c. Faith and love

Galatians 5:6

What is necessary for faith to work? _____

8. Hindrances to answered prayer

What type of things cause our prayers to be hindered?

a. Psalm 66:18 _____

b. Mark 11:25 _____

c. James 4:3 _____

d. 1 John 3:21,22 _____

e. 1 Peter 3:7 (If you are married, what could hinder your prayers?) _____

_____

B. PERSONAL APPLICATION

What is your plan for daily prayer? It is helpful to schedule a specific time each day when you will meet with the Lord and share with Him from your heart. You may want to start your prayer life by using some of the suggestions listed below.

To get into the habit of daily prayer, you may want to start a systematic program and keep a daily prayer journal. As you become more comfortable in prayer, you will depend more upon the Holy Spirit and less on lists and programs. However, many times in the initial stages of developing your prayer life, some prayer tools can help you develop discipline and consistency in your prayer life.

Daily Prayer Suggestions:

Praise and worship God for Who He is.

Thank God for what He has done and for what He will do.

Confess any known sin.

Make specific requests for yourself and others.

You may want to make a list of those you want to pray for. Your list might include the following:

> government leaders
>
> ministers (pastors, missionaries, workers)
>
> fellow Christians
>
> enemies
>
> non-Christians
>
> personal needs

C. GROUP EXERCISE

Scripture prayers to pray:

God has given us anointed prayers in His Word. We can pray these prayers for ourselves and others, and we are guaranteed to get results. The Holy Spirit inspired the apostle Paul and others to pray certain prayers that are recorded in the New Testament. Use these prayers as a pattern for your own prayers. To pray these prayers for yourself and others, simply insert your name (or another's) in these prayers. You will see dynamic results!

As a group, look up the following Scriptures and pray these prayers for one another.

Ephesians 1:17-20

Ephesians 3:14-20

Colossians 1:9-12

Philippians 1:9-12

CHAPTER FIVE

HOW TO HEAR FROM GOD

A. HOW DOES GOD TALK TO ME?

God's Word, the Bible, is God's personal love letter to you. As you read the Bible, you will sense that God Himself is whispering in your spiritual ear, and indeed He is! The Bible is unlike any other book because it is alive and full of life and power. It is your primary source of spiritual food. It will help you to grow and to be strong. Because the Bible will give you spiritual food, strength, light and power, the enemy will do anything he can to distract you from reading it. Your Bible will teach you everything you need to know to walk victoriously in this life. It is no wonder he fights so hard to keep you from reading it. Schedule a daily reading time into your life right now. Let's take a look at this exciting Book, the Bible.

1. Who wrote the Bible?

   a. The Bible is a supernaturally written Book.

      2 Timothy 3:16,17

      Who do the Scriptures say inspired the writing of the Bible? _____

      2 Peter 1:20,21

      Is any part of the Scripture not inspired by God?_____

   b. Jesus believed that the Scriptures were inspired by God, because He consistently quoted the Old Testament as His authority.

      John 5:39

      Who do the Scriptures testify about? _____

      John 5:46,47

      Who was Moses writing about in the Old Testament? _____

2. How reliable is the Bible?

   Will the Bible ever become obsolete? What do these verses tell us about the Bible?

   a. Psalm 119:89 _____

b. Matthew 24:35 _____

c. 1 Peter 1:25 _____

d. Isaiah 40:8 _____

A SUPERNATURAL BOOK: The Bible was written by forty different men who had various occupations. It was written during a period of more than 1,500 years in three languages (Hebrew, Aramaic, and Greek). The Bible has one consistent central theme in both the Old and New Testaments: Jesus Christ. It is obvious to any reader that there is one Supreme Author of the Bible, the Holy Spirit of God.

3. Why did God give us the Bible?

    2 Timothy 3:16,17

    a. What does the Scripture provide for the believer? _____

    _____

    _____

    b. What is the result for every believer? _____

    _____

4. What does God's Word do in our lives?

    a. Hebrews 4:12 _____

    _____

    b. John 8:31,32 _____

    c. John 15:3 _____

    d. Psalm 119:105 _____

    e. Psalm 119:130 _____

    f. 2 Peter 1:4 _____

    g. Psalm 19:7,8 _____

    What four things does the Word of God do for us? _____

    _____

_____

_____

5. How does God's Word help us grow?

 a. God's Word — our spiritual food

   Our physical body needs food to grow and to be strong. The same is true for our spirit. We cannot grow if we do not *eat* God's Word. Our spiritual growth will be sporadic if we only *snack* on the Word occasionally. We need a constant diet of God's Word. What is the Bible compared to?

   Matthew 4:4 _____

   1 Peter 2:2 _____

   Psalm 119:103 _____

 b. God's Word — likened to a seed

   A seed must be planted into soil before it can grow. In the same way, the Word of God must be planted into your heart in order for you to grow spiritually. Jesus described four different types of soil, or heart conditions, which received the seed of God's Word and the results of each type. The various soil types are listed below. Describe what happened when the seed was sown in each heart.

   Luke 8:4-15

   the way side _____

   _____

   rocky ground _____

   _____

   thorny ground _____

   _____

   good ground _____

   _____

6. What is our responsibility?

What are we instructed to do with the Word?

a. Colossians 3:16 _____

b. 2 Timothy 2:15_____

c. Psalm 119:11_____

What is the result? _____

d. Joshua 1:8

When are we to meditate? _____

What are the results of meditating? _____

_____

e. Psalm 1:1,2_____

7. What are the results of hearing God's Word?

a. Romans 10:17 _____

b. James 1:22-25

After we have heard the Word, what are we told to do?_____

What happens if we hear God's Word but do not do it?_____

Compare looking into a mirror and looking into God's Word...

What is the purpose and result of both? _____

_____

What happens if we hear God's Word and do it?_____

_____

c. John 14:21

When we obey God's Word what are we telling Jesus?_____

Can we love Jesus without obeying His commands? _____

8. Who helps us understand the Word?

a. John 14:26 _____

b. John 16:13 _____

c. 1 Corinthians 2:11-13 _____

9. God's Word is one of our weapons.

God has not left us helpless against the enemy. He has given us one of the strongest weapons available to overcome all of the devil's attacks. What weapon is the Word of God likened to?

a. Ephesians 6:17 _____

b. Hebrews 4:12 _____

c. Matthew 4:1-11 _____

When the devil tried to tempt Jesus, Jesus overcame him by using God's Word, the Sword of the Spirit. What three words did Jesus consistently use to thwart the devil's temptations?

_____

What was He quoting? _____

B. PERSONAL APPLICATION

Do you have a daily Bible reading plan? _____

If not, purchase or design your own systematic plan whereby you can read the Bible each day. Perhaps your goal can be to read at least one or more chapters in the Bible each day. You might also consider one of the following plans to enhance your study of God's Word.

1. Study the Bible using workbooks, concordances and other reference materials.

2. Take notes of the pastor's sermon each Sunday.

3. Listen to teaching tapes.

4. Read faith-building material.

5. Attend seminars and conferences where the Word is preached.

C. GROUP EXERCISE

As a group, have each person share a Scripture verse or passage that has recently had personal meaning to them.

As a group, you might want to take time to outline one of the Epistles in the New Testament.

CHAPTER SIX

HOW TO OBEY GOD

A. SHOW GOD YOU LOVE HIM

Walking with God includes the element of obedience to God. God is not a harsh taskmaster, nor a short-fused judge. He is a loving Father. If we know God loves us and that He has our best interest in mind, we can easily trust and obey Him.

1. Why should we obey God?

   a. Acts 5:29

   With so many voices clamoring for our attention and allegiance, why should we obey God? _____

   b. 1 John 4:8

   What does this verse tell us about God? _____

   _____

   If God is love, how does that help us obey Him?_____

   c. 1 John 4:18

   How does the first part of this verse make it easy to obey God?_____

2. How do we show God that we love Him?

   a. John 14:15

   What did Jesus say was the real test of true love for God?_____

   b. John 14:21,23,24

   According to verse 21, who really loves God? _____

   _____

   Can you love God and not obey Him? _____

   If you don't obey God, what are you saying to Him? _____

3. Is it really possible to obey God?

    a. 1 John 5:3

        Are God's commandments too hard to obey? _____

    b. Philippians 2:13

        Who helps us obey? _____

    c. Philippians 4:13

        Is there anything we can't do with Christ's help? _____

        As we seek to please God, He works in us both the desire to want His will and the ability to do His will.

4. What commandments are we to obey?

In the Old Testament, the children of Israel were instructed to obey the Ten Commandments as well as other laws laid down by God. Under the New Testament God has summarized all of His laws into **two** commandments based on the new commandment of love. What do the Scriptures teach concerning this new commandment of love?

    a. John 13:34,35

        What is this new commandment? _____

        _____

    b. Matthew 22:36-40

        All the Law and prophets of the Old Testament can be summarized into what two commandments? _____

        _____

    c. Romans 13:8-10

        Under the New Testament, how are we to fulfill the law? _____

    d. John 15:12,17

        Jesus reiterated this commandment because it is so radically opposed to our selfish nature and our religious thinking. What is His commandment?_____

_____

e. James 2:8

In John's gospel, Jesus called "the law of love" a new commandment. In James' epistle, what is "the law of love" called? _____

f. 1 John 3:16-23

How are we to love? (vv. 16-18.) _____

_____

If our heart (or conscience) begins to condemn us, what is the first thing we need to check up on? (vv. 19-23.) _____

_____

If we walk in love, will our heart (or conscience) condemn us? (vv. 19-21.) _____

If we have a clear heart (or conscience) before God, what are we promised? (vv. 21,22.)

_____

g. Mark 11:25,26; Matthew 18:21-35

According to the above-listed passages, what is the biggest hindrance to obeying God's new commandment? _____

5. What are the benefits of obedience?

a. James 1:22-25

What is a person doing who hears the Word but does not obey it? _____

_____

What is a person promised who hears the Word and obeys it? _____

_____

b. John 15:10

What are we promised if we obey God's commandments? _____

c. Luke 6:46-49

Can you truly call Jesus your Lord and not obey His Word? _____

Let's compare the obedient and the disobedient hearer.	Obedient	Disobedient
Who heard the Word?		
Who obeyed the Word?		
Who faced the flood and storm?		
Whose house wasn't shaken?		
Whose house fell apart?		

What is the only difference between a Christian who stands strong and endures storms and a Christian who falls apart in the midst of storms? _____

_____

6. What are the practical ways to obey God?

As new Christians there are several areas of obedience that will be of great help to our spiritual growth. Keep in mind that obedience to God is not intended to put us back under some system of "good works" or under the law in order to obtain God's favor. God loves us in spite of us sometimes missing the mark.

Actually, obeying God is for our benefit, not God's. When we obey the Word of God, we are actually blessing ourselves. God is not up in heaven shaking His head and saying, "Tsk, tsk," when we are disobedient; rather, He is grieved because He knows the troubles we will face if we continue to disobey the guidelines He has written in the Bible which are intended for our well-being.

a. Obedience in seeking God first

Matthew 6:33

What are we to seek first? _____

What is the promised result? _____

_____

How does seeking God first and obeying God relate? _____

_____

b. Obedience in separation from the love of the world

1 John 2:15-17

What are we told not to love? _____

What does "the world" consist of? _____

_____

What is the destiny for "the world"? _____

What is the destiny for those who love God and do His will?_____

c. Obedience in forgetting the past

The enemy will oftentimes try to trip you up in your walk with God by reminding you of your past. If your past is full of sin and failure, then Satan will try to use that as a "ball and chain" of condemnation to keep you from moving forward.

If your past is full of success, Satan may also try to remind you of what you have "given up" in an attempt to keep you looking back at the so-called "good old time" instead of looking ahead to the high calling of God for your life.

Philippians 3:13,14

What are we supposed to forget? _____

_____

2 Corinthians 5:17

What happened to your old life?_____

Luke 9:62

Where did God say not to look? _____

Galatians 2:20

What happened to the "old" you?_____

Acts 19:18,19

What did these Christians do with the paraphernalia and reminders of their past life of sin? _____

d. Obedience in attending a good church

Hebrews 10:24,25

Relationships with other Christians are vital. What is God telling us not to neglect? ___

_____

Acts 2:42,46,47

This passage describes the first Christian church. What are some of the characteristics you should look for in a church? _____

_____

_____

1 Corinthians 15:33

Good friends and companions are important. As a new Christian, it is important that you make new friends who share your enthusiasm and love for Christ.

What does this verse say will happen if a person spends most of his or her time with ungodly people? _____

_____

Where can you meet good Christian friends?

_____

e. Obedience in water baptism

Water baptism is an outward demonstration of the inward work that God has done in you. Water baptism is an act of obedience in which you publicly declare to the world that your old life is dead and buried and your new life is now identified with Christ. Many people have been baptized as infants, or even as children, before they really made their own personal decision for Christ. The scriptural precedent for water baptism shows that this act of faith should take place **after** a person has confessed Jesus as his or her Lord.

Acts 8:12

Who was baptized? _____

When were they baptized? _____

Acts 8:36-38

What is the prerequisite for baptism? _____

_____

What was the eunuch baptized in? _____

Acts 18:8

What follows believing in Jesus? _____

f. Obedience in telling others about Jesus

On one hand, obedience to God involves separating yourself from the love of the world and ungodly companions. On the other hand, obedience to God involves going into the world to share Christ with those who do not know Him. You can be in this world and friendly to unsaved people, yet not be of the same spirit as the world. In fact, Jesus has instructed us to go into the world to tell others of His great love and forgiveness.

Mark 16:15

What is the last command Jesus gave before He was taken up into heaven? _____

_____

Matthew 28:19,20

Who is with us when we tell others of Jesus? _____

_____

Acts 1:8

Who helps us witness of Christ? _____

In a legal sense, what is a "witness"? _____

_____

_____

What is the best thing you could possibly tell anyone?_____

B. PERSONAL APPLICATION

Make a quality decision to change your thinking or behavior so that it lines up with God's Word. Are there areas of your life that you need to bring into obedience to God?_____

_____

What are the area(s) where you need to make changes? _____

_____

_____

What are you going to do to obey God?_____

_____

C. GROUP EXERCISE

How do we walk in love?

Look up the following passages and discuss ways you can begin to practice these things with the people with whom you come into contact every day. You might want to assign one or two passages to different people to study and memorize. Ask those people, then, to lead the group discussion relating to their passages.

1 Corinthians 13:4-7   Philippians 2:1-4

Romans 12:10-18   Colossians 3:12-17

Matthew 5:43-48   John 4:7-11

Galatians 5:13-15

CHAPTER SEVEN

HOW TO EXPERIENCE GOD'S LOVE AND FORGIVENESS

Relationships are one of the joys of life. Talking to, working with and interacting with people are the nuts and bolts of everyday living. Our relationship with God is the most important relationship of all.

In the same way that we have been born into our natural families and have a relationship with our earthly fathers, so, too, we have been born into the family of God through Jesus Christ. We have a relationship with God the Father. Nothing can change our **blood** relationship with our earthly father, and nothing can change our **blood** relationship with our heavenly Father. Our relationship with God is secure because of the blood of Jesus Christ.

However, the **quality** of our relationship with people and the degree of closeness in friendships can vary depending upon the behavior of the people involved. We can see this through the following example of a situation that could occur in a father-child relationship.

Suppose you are a teenager who has just received your driver's license. It's Friday night and your father gives you the keys to the new car. At midnight, you return home after a fun evening with your friends. You confidently pull the car into the driveway, only to hear the sickening sound of the scraping metal. Your heart sinks as you realize that you have just hit the mailbox with your dad's new car! You park the car in the garage and immediately check the rear bumper for damages. To your surprise, there isn't a scratch on the car. You look to heaven and whisper a heartfelt, "Thank You, Lord."

You quietly walk out to inspect the damaged mailbox. You slip into the house and tiptoe upstairs. As you fall off to sleep you are battling with the question, "Should I tell Dad?" The next morning you decide not to mention anything about the mailbox. Since there wasn't any damage to the car, your dad will assume some vandals sideswiped the mailbox during the night. Besides, if you did tell your dad, maybe he wouldn't trust you with the car in the future.

What you don't know, however, is that your dad saw the whole incident! He was sitting in the darkened living room, looking out the picture window, waiting for you to arrive safely home. He saw you knock out the mailbox. He saw you check the mailbox. He saw it all. At breakfast, he is waiting for you to tell him all about it. When you don't say anything about it, how do you think that affects your relationship with him?

A. RELATIONSHIP VERSUS FRIENDSHIP

Answer the following questions based on the incident described in the car/mailbox illustration above.

1. How do you think the father feels? _____

2. How do you think the child-parent *friendship* has been affected? Do they still have close fellowship?_____

3. How do you think the child-parent *relationship* has been affected? Do they still have a father-child relationship? _____

4. What should the teenager do if he wants to restore their friendship? _____

5. What do you think will happen to the friendship if the teenager never says anything to his father about the mailbox? _____

_____

6. Do you think the father still loves his child? _____

7. Our relationship with our heavenly Father is similar to our relationship with our earthly father. Our heavenly Father knows everything we think and sees everything we do. God loves us and is willing to forgive us if we will be honest and confess our sin to Him. Read 1 John 1:6-10 and see what parallels you can draw from this story. _____

_____

_____

_____

B. HOW DOES GOD SEE ME?

God the Father loves us more than our earthly father does, and He has given us certain instructions to obey. These instructions are not intended to restrict us or to keep us from having fun; they are actually for our good. God knows what is best for us, and His commandments are designed to enable us to live life to the fullest.

Although the quality of our friendship with God can change according to our behavior, our right standing with God is not based on our goodness or on our behavior. Our right standing with God is based solely upon the love of God and the blood of Jesus. How does God see us?

1. 2 Corinthians 5:21

   According to this verse, what are we made? _____

_____

RIGHTEOUSNESS: Righteousness is a big religious-sounding word, but its meaning is very simple. The righteousness that God bestows upon us is simply the ability to stand before Him without any sense of guilt or inferiority, as though we have never sinned. God credits us with His righteousness.

How righteous is God? _____

2. Hebrews 10:14

When Jesus offered Himself for our sins, what did this do for us in God's sight? _____

_____

3. Hebrews 10:17

Is God keeping a record of your sins?_____

4. 1 John 1:7

As we walk in the light of God's Word, what does the blood of Jesus do for us? _____

_____

5. Romans 8:1

To whom does this verse say there is no condemnation? _____

Like a father, God loves His children. He does not condemn us or hold a grudge against us. At the same time, however, God is not a spineless mass of spiritual mush, either. He does not wink at sin, but He offers forgiveness to those who will confess and forsake it.

C. HOW DOES GOD DEFINE SIN?

1. 1 John 3:4 _____

THE LAW: As we have seen in the previous chapter, the law referred to here is the law of love.

2. James 4:17 _____

3. 1 John 5:17 _____

4. Romans 14:23_____

D. WHO SINS?

1 John 1:8,10_____

E. WHO TEMPTS US TO SIN?

1. Matthew 4:1

   Who is at the ultimate root of all sin? _____

2. James 1:13-15

   Who never tempts us to sin? _____

   Through what does the devil tempt us? _____

   _____

   When does temptation become sin? _____

   _____

TEMPTATION: It is important to remember that temptation is not sin. To be tempted is normal for the Christian. Jesus was tempted by the devil in the wilderness, and yet, we know that He never sinned. When you are tempted, don't let the enemy make you feel as if you have already sinned. Resist the temptation, and you will not sin.

   What is the result of sin? _____

F. HOW CAN WE RESIST THE TEMPTATION TO SIN?

1. 1 Corinthians 10:13

   Are the temptations you face unique? _____

   Does God ever allow you to be tempted with more than you can bear? _____

   What does God always provide? _____

   Is there ever any excuse for sin? _____

   Describe a temptation you have faced and identify the way of escape that was available to you. _____

   _____

   _____

_____

2. Proverbs 4:14,15

We can "nip sin in the bud" by avoiding certain relationships. What relationships are we to avoid?_____

When we are presented with an opportunity to sin, what does verse 15 say we should do?

_____

3. James 4:7

What does this verse tell us to do in relationship to the devil? _____

What will the devil do? _____

4. Joshua 7:20,21

What tempted Achan to sin? _____

When could Achan have escaped the temptation?_____

_____

What role did Achan's eyes play in his ultimate sin? _____

Describe the role of our eyes in yielding to or avoiding temptation. _____

_____

_____

G. WHAT DO WE DO IF WE SIN?

1. 1 John 1:9

This verse has been called the Christian's "bar of soap." What are we to do, according to this verse? _____

To confess our sins means to say the same thing about our sin that God does. To confess our sins is to agree with God that our action or attitude was wrong.

According to this verse, what will God do?_____

_____

If we confess our sin, will God hold our sin against us? _____

2. Psalm 38:18

   What are we to do when we sin? _____

3. Psalm 32:1-5

   What happened to David when he did not confess his sin? (vv. 3,4.) _____

   _____

   What happened when David did confess his sin? (v. 5.) _____

   Have you ever experienced this? _____

   Describe how you felt when you knew you had sinned and were not right with God. ___

   _____

   _____

   Describe how you felt when you confessed your sin and received God's forgiveness. ____

   _____

4. Proverbs 28:13

   If you cover your sins, what results can you expect? _____

   _____

   If you confess your sins, what can you expect? _____

   _____

5. 1 John 1:7

   If we walk in the light of God's Word, in a right relationship with God and with others, what are we promised? _____

   _____

Can you see that God wants to forgive and cleanse you from all sin? There is no greater sense of liberty than to know you are right with God and that there is nothing standing between you and your heavenly Father.

Satan does not want us to experience that freedom. He often works on our minds and emotions with feelings of guilt or condemnation to make us feel as though we are not forgiven, as if God is holding our sin against us. We must receive our forgiveness by faith, based on the Word of God, and not on our feelings.

H. PERSONAL APPLICATION

It is so important to be honest before God. As you confess your sin before Him, you enjoy a loving friendship with the Lord. Unconfessed sin is like the sludge that clogs sewer pipes. Over a period of time, the sludge blocks the free flow of water.

Unconfessed sin, over a period of time, can block the flow of God's love, can cause a heart to harden toward God and develop a bitterness toward the things of God. The blood of Jesus continually cleanses us from all sin as we keep our hearts honest and pure before God.

Take a moment and apply 1 John 1:9 to your life, right now. If there are areas of your life where you have sinned and have not confessed them to the Lord, write them down on a piece of paper. Now, read 1 John 1:9. After you confess those sins and ask God to forgive you, write "1 John 1:9" across that piece of paper as an act of your faith and say out loud, "All of these sins are now forgiven, and I am cleansed from all unrighteousness!" Now tear that piece of paper into tiny pieces and throw those pieces away, never to be remembered. This is exactly what God does with your sin. He will remember them no more!

I. GROUP EXERCISE

Read Psalm 51:1-12 and discuss David's honesty before God.

Did David try to blame someone else for his sin?

Against Whom did David say he had sinned?

What was David's prayer after he had received forgiveness?

CHAPTER EIGHT

HOW TO BE FILLED WITH THE HOLY SPIRIT

As a new believer, you have been growing in your relationship with the Lord, getting to know the goodness of your heavenly Father and discovering that Jesus is your Friend. Are you hungry for more of God? How well do you know the Holy Spirit? Maybe you've wondered how you could get to know the Holy Spirit better. He is a very real person. Let's look at how we can be full of the Spirit.

A. WHO IS THE HOLY SPIRIT?

As we have stated previously, the Holy Spirit is the third person of the Godhead or Trinity. The Trinity is made up of the Father, Son and Holy Spirit. The Holy Spirit is a person, not an "it" or an impersonal "force."

Acts 5:3,4

In verse 4, with Whom does Peter equate the Holy Spirit?_____

B. WHAT DOES IT MEAN TO BE *FILLED WITH THE HOLY SPIRIT?*

1. Understanding the two definitions

There is a difference between being born of the Spirit (the Spirit coming within our spirit) and being filled with the Holy Spirit (the Spirit coming upon our spirit). Let's look at the following examples:

a. John 3:5

Jesus said that unless a person is born of water and _____, he cannot enter the kingdom of God.

b. Acts 2:4

After the believers were_____, they began to speak in tongues as the Spirit gave them utterance.

c. John 14:17

Jesus said the Holy Spirit would dwell with us and shall be _____ us. (This happens when you are born again.)

d. Acts 1:8

   Jesus also said that the Holy Spirit would come _____ us. (This happens when you are filled with the Holy Spirit.)

2. Understanding the two experiences

The Scriptures teach that there are two experiences for the believer.

   a. First and foremost is the experience of salvation, or the new birth. When a person believes in his heart and confesses with his mouth that Jesus is Lord and that God raised Him from the dead, he receives the gift of salvation or eternal life. At this point, a person is **born of** the Spirit and is made a new creation in Christ. We could say he receives the Spirit within. In other words, the Holy Spirit recreates the human spirit and dwells **within** our spirit.

   b. Second, the experience subsequent to salvation is known in the Scriptures as **being filled** with the Holy Spirit, **receiving** the Holy Spirit, or **being baptized** with the Holy Spirit. When this happens, the believer is endued with power for service. We could say the Holy Spirit comes upon our spirit and endues us with power.

3. Understanding two extreme teachings

Sometimes a new believer can become confused by the various teachings concerning the Holy Spirit. Like any spiritual matter, there can be a "ditch" on either side of the road. As a wise believer, you will want to stay out of the ditch on either side and stay safely in the middle of the road on solid biblical truth. What are the two extremes concerning the work of the Holy Spirit in the life of a believer?

   a. Extreme #1: There is no such thing as an experience subsequent to salvation called being filled, receiving, or being baptized with the Holy Spirit.

   b. Extreme #2: Unless a person is filled or baptized in the Holy Spirit subsequent to salvation, he does not have the Holy Spirit at all.

   Actually, the Scriptures teach that there is an experience of being filled or baptized in the Spirit subsequent to salvation. But the Bible does not teach that unless a person is filled, or baptized, with the Holy Spirit, he or she does not have the Holy Spirit at all.

C. THE DIFFERENCE BETWEEN *BORN OF* AND *FILLED WITH* THE HOLY SPIRIT

The difference between being born of the Spirit (the experience of salvation) and being filled with the Spirit (the experience of being baptized with the Spirit) is examined in the following Scriptures:

1. "Born of the Spirit" — baptized into the Body of Christ

   1 Corinthians 12:13

   Who is the Baptizer in this verse? _____

   Who is being baptized? _____

   What are we being baptized into? _____

BAPTIZED: It means "to dip into" or "to immerse."

2. "Filled with the Spirit" — baptized with the Holy Spirit

   Luke 3:16 (the second half of this verse)

   Who is the Baptizer in the last part of the verse? _____

   Who would He baptize? _____

   What are we being baptized with? _____

We can see from these Scriptures that the Holy Spirit baptizes us and places us into the Body of Christ, immediately, at the time of our salvation, or new birth. This is something that happens automatically to every believer in Jesus Christ. The Lord Jesus then baptizes us with the Holy Spirit, subsequent to our new birth. This infilling of the Spirit is available to every believer who desires more of God. Jesus, in fact, in Acts 1:4,5 commands all believers to be baptized in the Holy Ghost.

D. COMPARING THE TWO EXPERIENCES

Salvation is the baptism into the Body of Christ. The baptism in the Holy Spirit occurs when Jesus fills us with the Holy Spirit and endows us with power for service.

First we are **born** of the Spirit when we receive Jesus as Lord; then, we are to be **filled** with the Spirit after we receive salvation.

Look at the passages below and place the words "born of the Spirit" or "filled with the Spirit" in the blank space to indicate which experience is depicted in the verse. We can clearly see these two experiences in the life of Jesus and other believers in these Scriptures.

1. Jesus

   Matthew 1:18-20 _____

Matthew 3:16 _____

2. Disciples

John 20:21,22 _____

Acts 1:2-5 _____

3. Samaritans

Acts 8:5,12 _____

Acts 8:14-17 _____

4. Ephesians

Acts 19:1-5 _____

Acts 19:6 _____

E. WHY SHOULD I BE FILLED WITH THE HOLY SPIRIT?

As a believer, you have already been born of the Spirit and placed into the Body of Christ. Why would you want the additional experience of being filled with the Holy Spirit?

1. God has commanded us

Ephesians 5:18

What are God's two words concerning the Holy Spirit? _____

This Scripture denotes the idea of continually being filled with the Spirit, to "be being filled." To stay full of the Spirit one would have to receive an *initial infilling,* and thereafter we are commanded to continue to be full of the Spirit.

2. We need power

Acts 1:8

What is the purpose for being filled with the Spirit? _____

F. HOW CAN A PERSON BE FILLED WITH THE SPIRIT?

1. First, be sure that you are born again.

If you are a believer, the Holy Spirit has already been at work in your life helping you receive Jesus as your Lord. Now you are ready to receive the Holy Spirit in His fullness.

Acts 2:38

What happens after you repent and are baptized into the Body of Christ? _____

_____

2. Second, simply ask and receive the Holy Spirit by faith.

Luke 11:9-13

What do verses 9 and 10 say will happen if you ask? _____

What does verse 13 say we can ask the Father for? _____

According to verses 11 and 12, if we ask the Father for one thing, will He give us something different? _____

If we ask for the Holy Spirit, what will we receive?

_____ a demon spirit

_____ an embarrassing gift

_____ a weird or spooky gift

_____ the Holy Spirit

God gave the Holy Spirit to all of mankind on the Day of Pentecost. When you ask the Father to fill you with the Holy Spirit, you are simply saying you want to receive what He has already given to mankind nearly 2,000 years ago.

3. Third, begin to yield to the Holy Spirit. (This will be discussed more fully in chapter 9.)

G. PERSONAL APPLICATION

1. Are you thirsty?

Jesus has made a river of living water available to every believer. (John 7:37-39.)

2. Are you ready to receive?

Take a moment to ask the Father in Jesus' name to fill you with the Holy Spirit. You may want to pray a prayer like this — pray it from your heart.

> Dear Father God, I ask You in Jesus' name to fill me with the Holy Spirit so that I may receive the fullness of Your Spirit. Lord, I want to have power to be a witness for You. I want to be able to praise You from my innermost being, and I want to speak Your Word boldly. Jesus, I believe You are the Baptizer, so I ask You to baptize me in the Spirit now. I believe I receive the Holy Spirit now. Thank You, Lord.

3. What should I expect?

Once you have asked God to fill you with the Spirit, believe that He has done it, just as He promised. You may sense the Spirit coming upon you. You may begin to feel as if a river were bubbling up inside of you. You may feel as if you want to speak words you have never heard before. This is a manifestation of the Holy Spirit and is the evidence of the Holy Spirit's indwelling presence. Don't quench this supernatural utterance, but rather, yield to it and let this utterance of the Holy Spirit flow from your mouth. You are speaking praises to God in other tongues.

As you yield to the Spirit and begin to move your mouth and to use your vocal chords, allow yourself to flow in this spiritual language as the rivers of living water come up from your innermost being. You may sense the desire to speak a fluent language, or just one or two words that are foreign to you. Speak them out in faith and let the river begin to flow. As you quiet your mind and allow your spirit to release itself, you will begin to magnify God in tongues you have never learned.

What if you don't "feel" anything? What if you don't "feel" a river bubbling up on the inside of you? Remember, feelings have nothing to do with Bible facts. If you have asked God to baptize you in the Spirit, then believe He has done just exactly that. Expect the evidence of speaking in tongues as the Scriptures teach, and you will sense that river bubbling up inside of you. Simply yield to the Spirit, and you will begin to speak in other tongues. As you worship God, your English vocabulary will be inadequate, and you will find yourself speaking words you have never learned.

We receive the Spirit by *faith*. We speak in other tongues as we *yield* to the Holy Spirit.

In the next chapter, we will study the scriptural purpose for speaking in tongues.

H. GROUP EXERCISE

As a group, you can take this opportunity to pray for one another to be filled with the Spirit. First, spend time worshipping God together. Then the group leader can pray and lay hands on those who desire to be filled with the Spirit.

As a group, maintain an expectant and reverent attitude toward the Lord. As you focus on Him, you may begin to sing aloud as a group, in English and in other tongues, as each one is filled with the Spirit.

It is important that no one feel any pressure or any embarrassment, but that the love and presence of God are allowed to permeate your time together.

Because this is such an important time in the life of every believer, this time should not be rushed. Take time to worship God the Father, Jesus, the Son and the Holy Spirit from your heart of hearts.

CHAPTER NINE

HOW TO BE SURE YOU ARE FILLED WITH THE SPIRIT

There are many benefits of being filled with the Spirit. The initial evidence of being filled with the Spirit is to speak in other tongues. This is not the only evidence of being filled with the Spirit, but it is the initial manifestation of being filled with the Spirit.

In addition to this initial evidence of being filled with the Spirit, you will notice that you are receiving more light and revelation as you study God's Word. You will experience a new boldness and power in witnessing. The presence of God in your heart and your expression of praise and worship will take on new meaning. These are just a few of the benefits of being filled with the Spirit.

In this chapter we are going to concentrate our study on the initial evidence of being filled with the Spirit which is to speak in other tongues.

A. WHAT SHOULD I EXPECT?

Let's look at accounts in the book of Acts that describe believers being filled with the Spirit. What do these verses say happened when the New Testament believer received the Holy Spirit?

1. Acts 2:4 _____

2. Acts 10:44-46 _____

3. Acts 19:6 _____

Notice that the believers were speaking in tongues and magnifying God. When you receive the Holy Spirit you will have the supernatural ability to speak in other tongues. Sometimes, Christians have misunderstandings concerning the baptism of the Holy Spirit and the evidence of speaking in tongues. Many people have mistakenly interpreted the Word of God in this area by using their own understanding rather than leaning on God's Word and on His understanding.

B. DIFFERENT KINDS OF TONGUES

To the natural mind, speaking in tongues may seem silly. However, as you study the Word of God on this subject, you will see the great benefits of praying in tongues. Let's look at the Word and dismantle some of the myths concerning speaking in tongues.

What are the different kinds of tongues described in the New Testament?

1. 1 Corinthians 13:1

Tongues of _____ and of _____

2. 1 Corinthians 12:10

_____ kinds of tongues

3. 1 Corinthians 12:28

_____ of tongues

C. WHAT IS THE PURPOSE OF SPEAKING IN TONGUES?

Many people have lumped all speaking in tongues together into one basket, so to speak, but we can see from Scripture that there are at least two different purposes for speaking in tongues.

The first purpose for speaking in tongues that we can see in the Word of God is the "gift of tongues" which is used for ministry purposes in the local congregation. This gift of tongues requires an interpretation. This might also be called the public manifestation of tongues. This manifestation is used, as the apostle Paul said, for ministry "in the church."

Another purpose for speaking in tongues is for personal ministry or edification. This might be called the private manifestation of tongues and does not necessarily require an interpretation. This manifestation is available for every believer, as the apostle Paul said, "to edify himself."

In the Scriptures listed below, place the word "public" or "private" in the blank space to describe which manifestation of tongues the particular verse implies.

1. 1 Corinthians 12:28-30 _____

2. 1 Corinthians 14:2 _____

3. 1 Corinthians 14:14,15 _____

4. 1 Corinthians 14:26 _____

5. 1 Corinthians 14:4 _____

6. 1 Corinthians 14:18 _____

D. WHAT ARE THE BENEFITS OF SPEAKING IN TONGUES?

Have you ever wanted to praise the Lord from your innermost being? Have you ever wanted to thank God for all He has done for you? Have you ever wanted to talk to God "heart to heart," but you couldn't seem to find the right words? Sometimes our English language is so limited when we want to praise, thank or talk to the Lord.

At these times, speaking in tongues is of great benefit. The Holy Spirit helps us talk to God from our heart of hearts, through speaking in tongues. Speaking in tongues is also called "a prayer language," or "praying or speaking in the Spirit." When we exercise this prayer language, we are literally by-passing our mind and intellect, and we are praying straight from our spirit to God.

Speaking to God in our prayer language is like having a direct hotline to God, and our prayer, or speech, is not clouded by our thoughts, emotions or feelings. As we pray in the Spirit in tongues, we receive a great spiritual blessing.

1. 1 Corinthians 14:2

   Who are we speaking to when we pray in tongues? _____

   _____

   When we pray in tongues, we have a direct hotline...straight to God!

2. 1 Corinthians 14:4

   What happens to someone who prays in tongues? _____

   _____

EDIFY: "To charge up." Just like charging up a battery, our spirit will be charged or built up with strength and power as we pray in tongues.

3. Jude 20

   How do we build ourselves up on our most holy faith? _____

PRAYING IN THE HOLY GHOST: One of the best habits you can get into early in your Christian life is that of praying in the Holy Ghost. Pray in tongues, not as a mindless exercise but with the awareness that as you pray in tongues you are literally charging up your spirit and building yourself up on your most holy faith.

Your mind may not understand it and, for that reason, you may be tempted to avoid praying in tongues. But if you will determine to pray in tongues by faith, whether you understand it or not, you will find yourself receiving great spiritual edification and blessing.

4. Romans 8:26

   Have you ever needed to pray about something, but you didn't know how to pray? _____

GROANINGS WHICH CANNOT BE UTTERED: One meaning of this phrase, according to P. C. Nelson, noted linguist and Bible doctrine scholar and author, is "groanings that cannot be uttered in articulate speech." In other words, the groanings can be in a language which our intellect doesn't comprehend; that is, other tongues.

What will the Holy Spirit do for us as we speak in tongues?_____

E. COMMON MISUNDERSTANDINGS CONCERNING TONGUES

1. Is it true that not everyone has "the gift of tongues"?

It is true that not everyone has the **public** gift of tongues for ministry in a congregation; however, this is not true concerning the **private** use of tongues for spiritual edification. The private manifestation of tongues is available to everyone, as seen in 1 Corinthians 14:5 where Paul says he would desire for all of us to speak in tongues.

It is clear that Paul is advocating the private use of tongues for personal edification as he had explained in verse 4. However, in the church (in public) he would rather have us prophesy — or speak in tongues with the interpretation. This operation of the public manifestation of the gift of tongues is as the Spirit wills, and everyone does not have this gift.

2. Is there any scriptural basis for "praying or singing in tongues"?

Often, because the Word has been misunderstood in this area, many people have not seen the scriptural basis for what is sometimes called "praying in the Spirit," or a "private prayer language." Notice in 1 Corinthians 14:14,15, Paul said he could "pray in an unknown tongue." Praying in unknown tongues is distinct from speaking in tongues with an interpretation. Praying in tongues is scriptural. Prayer is something that is done privately, or possibly in a group prayer setting, and is different than giving a public utterance in tongues with an interpretation. A person may, or may not, interpret what he prays in tongues. Paul encourages us, however, in 1 Corinthians 14:13, to pray that we may interpret.

Paul went on to explain that when he was praying in the Spirit his spirit prayed and his understanding was unfruitful. When he prayed in the Spirit, or in other tongues, it came from his spirit and his mind did not understand what he was saying. Notice, he also included the personal benefit of singing in the Spirit, or singing in other tongues. To pray and sing in the Spirit — in other tongues — for personal edification is, indeed, scriptural. It is important to mention that, according to 1 Corinthians 14:2, when we speak in unknown tongues for our personal benefit, we are speaking to God, not to men, and not to the devil. When we speak in our prayer language, we are edifying ourselves. This ability to speak in other tongues is available to every Spirit-filled believer and is a different manifestation of speaking in tongues than what is called the gift of tongues for use in the public assembly, which requires an interpretation.

3. Our church doesn't believe in speaking in tongues.

It is good to respect your church's beliefs and doctrine. However, if your church's beliefs and doctrine ever conflict with the written Word of God, then you need to take sides with the Word of God. Consider this: Jesus referred to believers speaking in tongues when He gave the Great Commission to the Universal Church in Mark 16:17. In 1 Corinthians 14:39 Paul said, **Forbid not to speak with tongues.**

4. I was taught tongues have passed away and are no longer in use.

Some churches teach that when the disciples passed away and when the New Testament was written, the "perfect" came, and tongues ceased, according to 1 Corinthians 13:8-10. First, we need to look at what is meant by the word "perfect." Consider this: If that which is "perfect" has come and tongues have ceased, then, according to this particular passage of Scripture, prophecy and knowledge also would have ceased. We know, however, that knowledge has not ceased but, in fact, it has actually increased. Therefore, we know that the "perfect" has not come, yet. The "perfect" shall come when He, the perfect One, appears in His Second Coming. Until that time comes, tongues, prophecy and knowledge are still with us.

5. I'm afraid if I speak in tongues it will get out of control.

This is a common fear. Some people think that the Holy Spirit will force them to speak in tongues and cause them to blurt out in tongues at some inopportune time. This is a fallacy.

Paul clearly says in 1 Corinthians 14:32 that the spirits of the prophets are subject to the prophets. In other words, you have control over your spirit and mouth. God never forces anyone to do anything. He will never embarrass you by causing you to speak in tongues beyond your control. A person can always control the starting and stopping of speaking in tongues. God will never violate your free will.

6. Will the Holy Spirit take over my mouth?

No. Acts 2:4 shows us that **They were all filled with the Holy Ghost, and [they] began to speak with other tongues, as the Spirit gave them utterance.** The Holy Spirit will not take over your mouth. You will do the speaking. The Holy Spirit will give you the utterance. You may feel a sensation in your vocal chords, or you may feel like expressing certain words, or you may have a sense of wanting to talk in what may sound like "baby talk," but you do the speaking. Sometimes there may seem to be one or two words, or maybe a whole sentence, just bubbling up from within you. When you simply yield to that, you will begin to speak in tongues.

7. I'm afraid a demon might speak through me instead of the Holy Spirit.

This also is a common fear. Perhaps the devil uses this thought to keep people from speaking in tongues because he himself fears the power of God released through people who speak in tongues. You can be comforted to know that you will receive a good gift from God, not a demon. Jesus assures us in Luke 11:9-13 that if we ask the Father for the Holy Spirit, He will not give us something else. Read this passage for yourself and see the goodness of God.

8. Do I have to "tarry" for the Holy Spirit?

No. In Luke 24:49, the disciples were told to "tarry," or to wait, until they were endued with power — the power of the Holy Spirit. Jesus said this to them because the Holy Spirit had not yet been given, or poured out, on the Church. On the Day of Pentecost, the Holy Spirit was sent by Jesus to the Church. We don't have to tarry, or wait, for this great event today because He has already come. We simply receive Him by faith.

9. Does someone have to lay hands on me and pray?

Not necessarily. There are different ways to receive the Holy Spirit, but the main element to receiving the Holy Spirit is to ask and believe. There is a scriptural precedent for receiving the Holy Spirit simply by hearing the Word of God and receiving. There is also scriptural precedent for asking God and receiving without the laying on of hands. In any case, it may help some people release their faith to receive the Holy Spirit when hands are laid on them, but it is not an absolute necessity.

10. Speaking in tongues seems so silly.

To our natural mind, speaking in tongues may seem silly. Our minds naturally want to know and understand everything. However, we have to remember that God is a Spirit, not a mind, and sometimes our minds will not comprehend spiritual things. Perhaps that is why Paul said in 1 Corinthians 1:27, **But God hath chosen the foolish things of the world to confound the wise; and God hath chosen the weak things of the world to confound the things which are mighty.**

F. PERSONAL APPLICATION

1 Corinthians 14:15

1. How did Paul say that he would pray?

_____ and _____

2. How did Paul say that he would sing?

_____ and _____

3. How will you sing and pray?

_____ and _____

4. Describe a time when you prayed in the Spirit or sang in the Spirit. What did you do? How did you feel afterwards? _____

_____

_____

_____

If you have never experienced this type of prayer, take time now to pray and sing to the Lord in other tongues.

G. GROUP EXERCISE

Study 1 Corinthians 14 and discuss the public and private manifestation of tongues, as Paul described them. As a group, take time to worship the Lord together in singing and speaking in tongues.

Ask God to teach you about the gift of tongues and about how to yield to the Holy Spirit in the operation of the public and private use of tongues. In a small group setting where the atmosphere is reverent and expectant, the Lord will manifest Himself in a very special way and will teach you how to flow with the Holy Spirit in this area.

CHAPTER 11

HOW TO EXPERIENCE THE ABUNDANT LIFE

A. GOD BLESS YOU

God wants you to experience a life of abundance. Remember that Jesus said in John 10:10: **I am come that they might have life, and that they might have it more abundantly.** What does it mean to experience abundance? What is abundant life? We know that abundant life begins when we receive Jesus Christ as our Lord, and we are born again. This is the beginning of life as God intended it to be, but it does not stop there. The abundant life, by definition, means the abundant, God-kind of life. What kind of life does God have?

God wants you to prosper in your spirit, in your soul (which is your will and the mental and emotional part of your personality) and in your body. Abundant life includes spiritual fulfillment, mental and emotional peace and physical healing and prosperity. Sometimes Christians are given the false impression that poverty, lack, oppression, sickness and tragedy in the life of a Christian are signs of spirituality. This idea proposes that in His sovereignty God afflicts a Christian with abuses so the Christian will demonstrate more nobility and humility than he would have if his life had been one of blessing and abundance. Maybe you've heard believers say things like, "The Lord is using this disease to teach me something." "God must have had a reason for allowing us to have that accident." "This tragedy is God's way of getting my attention." Insurance companies even call tornadoes, hurricanes and natural disasters "acts of God." The Bible does not teach that.

When we use the phrase "God bless you," we have to ask ourselves, what are we really saying? Does God want Christians to be blessed? Let's look at the Scriptures.

1. John 10:10

    What type of life did Jesus say He came to bring? _____

Abundantly: "Superabundant (in quantity) or superior (in quality)." The implication is excessive and beyond measure. To have more, to have enough and to spare, increase, a surplus!¹

2. 3 John 2

    What did the Holy Spirit inspire the apostle John to wish for Christians? _____

    _____

3. Proverbs 10:22

What does God's blessing do for believers? _____

_____

What does "he addeth no sorrow with it" mean?_____

_____

Should we be ashamed, apologetic or feel guilty if we are blessed with abundance? _____

4. Deuteronomy 11:21

If we obey the Lord's command, He promises long life for us and our children. In addition, He says that our days can be like _____

_____

Describe what "days of heaven" would include. _____

_____

_____

Describe what "days of heaven" would not include._____

_____

Where did God say we could have days of heaven? _____

_____

Remember, for a Christian the command that we are under in the New Covenant is the commandment to love — to love God and to love one another. If we walk in the law of love, we will qualify for "days of heaven" on the earth.

5. Psalm 103:1-5

In verse 2, what are we to remember? _____

_____

What benefits are listed in these verses? _____

_____

_____

6. Psalm 68:19

What does God want to "load" us with? _____

How often? _____

Is there any doubt that God wants believers to be blessed with abundant life? _____

B. WHY DOES GOD WANT US TO BE BLESSED WITH ABUNDANCE?

There are two basic reasons God wants us to experience the blessing of the abundant life.

First: God loves us and wants us to enjoy life.

Second: God loves others, and He wants us to be a channel so He can bless others through us.

God wants y...   ~ e a blessing.

It's a fact that the more y...   ...ritual and material things — the more you can give to others.

1. 1 Timothy 6:17,18

    God admonishes the rich to be aware of two things. This Scripture tells us that "God gives us richly all things." For what purpose?

    Verse 17: _____

    Verse 18: _____

2. Deuteronomy 8:11-18

    As we (believers) prosper in life, we are told to remember a few things.

    Who gives us the power to get wealth? _____

    Why does He give us power to get wealth? _____

    _____

TO ESTABLISH HIS COVENANT: God has always wanted His people to prosper. In the Old Testament we see the incredible wealth, well-being and health of God's people. As people blessed of the Lord, their lives were a testimony of God's goodness, and they had the resources necessary to perpetuate God's covenant and to bear the truth of His Word.

God wanted His people under the Old Covenant to be blessed and prosperous. How much more does God want His people under the new and better covenant (Heb. 8:6) to be blessed with abundance? As Christians are blessed, our lives testify to the generous nature of our heavenly Father. In addition, the Body of Christ then has the resources necessary to proclaim the good news of the Gospel around the world.

3. 2 Corinthians 9:7,8

Whom does God love? _____

Is God able to help you so that you will have plenty for enjoying life and plenty to give to others? _____

4. Matthew 6:33

What does this verse tell us? _____

_____

When it comes to abundance, blessings, prosperity and divine health, we need to keep our heart attitudes right. At times Christians can be caught up in greed, covetousness, selfishness and pride. If we aren't careful, we may begin to think God's Word is a "get rich quick" scheme or that we can use God's Word to parade our *health and wealth faith.* This is a dangerous way to think and believe. The Bible teaches us that the **love of money is the root of all evil** (1 Tim. 6:10). Pride, including spiritual pride, goes before destruction and a haughty spirit before a fall. (Prov. 16:18.) Our motives must be pure, holy and righteous. When our desire for the life of abundance is in order to advance God's plan and His will *first*, we are in position to receive His abundant blessings. Believers who are walking in the light of God's Word and in His law of love are in position to receive.

C. WE MUST LEARN TO BE CONTENT

While God does want us blessed, at the same time, He wants us to be content in all circumstances. We are to expect and look forward to God's great blessings while being content with our current lot in life. This is not always easy. Trust God for an increasing measure of the abundant life, and don't allow yourself to grumble with discontent in your present status in life.

1. Philippians 4:11-13

What did Paul say he had learned? (v. 11.) _____

_____

2. 1 Timothy 6:6

GODLINESS + _____ = GREAT GAIN

3. Hebrews 13:5

Concerning contentment, what does God tell us in this verse? _____

_____

To be content does not mean you have to forfeit your desire or your faith for all the blessings God's Word promises. It simply means that while you are in faith for the blessings of God, learn to be content until they are manifested.

D. TWO AREAS OF ABUNDANT LIVING: HEALING AND PROSPERITY

The subjects of divine healing, health and prosperity have caused no small stir among churches and denominations. Those who believe in healing and prosperity through faith have been labeled the "health and wealth" believers, the "name it and claim it" group, the "confess it and possess it" Christians. While there have been abuses in these areas by misguided Christians, there is a solid biblical basis for believing that God Himself wants believers healed and healthy in their bodies and prosperous in material and financial matters.

You might wonder, *If it is God's will for Christians to be healed and prosperous, why are so many Christians sick and poor?* Perhaps these thoughts will shed some light on the subject.

The Bible teaches that God is not willing that anyone perish, but that all should come to repentance. God loved the world so much that He sent His only Son that whosoever would believe in Him would not perish but would have everlasting life. (John 3:16.) It is God's will for all to be saved. Yet, we know that not everyone will be saved. Why? Simply because they refuse to believe God's Word; they refuse to believe in and receive Jesus Christ as Lord.

In the same way, we can see that the Bible teaches us it is God's will for all believers to have life and have it more abundantly. God wants us to prosper and be in health as our soul prospers. It is God's will for all believers to enjoy the abundant life — which includes healing and prosperity. Yet, we know that not everyone will experience healing, health and prosperity. Why? Many Christians refuse to believe God's Word on the subject. Many Christians would rather believe their experience, or the experience of other Christians, than to base their beliefs on God's Word.

On the other hand, there are times when believers do believe God's Word on the subject, but they are still not living in total health and prosperity. Why is this? There can be various reasons, but let's look at a few common reasons.

One reason could simply be a demonic attack in the areas of healing and prosperity. If the devil can defeat a Christian in these areas and "wear down" their faith, then he has accomplished a double victory. First, the Christian who became weary in well-doing, and who cast away his or her confidence in God's Word in these areas does not experience the blessing of healing and good health, nor abundant prosperity. Second, the devil has successfully silenced this Christian from preaching or ministering to others in these areas. There is no doubt that in these areas the Christian must patiently fight the good fight of faith to obtain the promises. It is not always easy to do, and oftentimes takes perseverance and requires longsuffering.

Another reason could simply be a misunderstanding of, or impatience, with regard to the law of sowing and reaping. Although this chapter does not include an in-depth look at God's laws of giving and receiving; nonetheless, giving is the way to abundant living! We will reap what we sow. (For further study please see: Gen. 8:22, 2 Cor. 9:6, Gal. 6:7-9, Luke 6:38, Mal. 3:10,11.) As we tithe and give offerings to the work of God we are sowing into God's Kingdom. Like any seed that is planted, a period of time will usually pass before we see any evidence of that growing seed. It was growing all the time, but often we have to wait a season or two to see and reap the full harvest of our seed on a consistent basis. Of course, our harvest will be in direct proportion to the amount we have sown. Again, we shall reap if we don't faint. This too is an area where faith and patience must be exercised on a regular basis.

Let's look at the Scriptures a little more closely. Most Christians will agree that God has the power to do anything. God has the ability to heal and prosper anyone he chooses. The real question in the mind of many believers is this: Is it God's will to heal and prosper *everyone*? We know God is able, but is He willing? Can we prove from the Bible that it is God's will to heal and prosper every believer? Let's look at these Scriptures.

1. God's will is revealed in our redemption.

Galatians 3:13,14

What has Christ already redeemed us from? _____

_____

THE CURSE OF THE LAW: The term "the law" usually refers to the Pentateuch, the first five books of the Bible. According to these five books we can see that the curse of the law, or the result of breaking God's law, is threefold — poverty, sickness and eternal death. Jesus through His death, burial and resurrection redeemed us from this curse. In other words, He freed us from the bondage of poverty, the destruction of sickness and disease and the eternal separation from God, if we will only believe and have faith in Him as our Redeemer.

What do these Scriptures tell us could now come on the Gentiles (nonbelievers) through Jesus Christ? _____

THE BLESSING OF ABRAHAM: We can see from a study of Abraham's life that the promise of the blessing of Abraham was first given in Genesis 12:1-3,5. Ultimately through Abraham's seed the Lord Jesus Christ would be born. Through Jesus Christ all of mankind would be blessed. In addition, the blessing of Abraham included blessings on him personally — on his body, on his name, on his family — and through him to others. In observing Abraham's life we see him as a man blessed of the Lord. He was blessed with a healthy, long life, as noted in Genesis 24:1. He was very rich, as mentioned in Genesis 13:2 and 24:34,35. He was a blessing to others, and he tithed ten percent of all that he had, as described in Genesis 14:18-20. His family was blessed, and his son Isaac received the blessing of Abraham. We can clearly see the blessing of Abraham included **health** and **wealth**. That blessing of Abraham is for us today, because in Christ we are Abraham's seed and heirs according to the promise. (See Galatians 3:16,29.)

2. What about sickness and poverty?

Deuteronomy 28

a. Deuteronomy 28:1-14

Beginning in verse 2, God categorizes the things He calls blessings. In our modern language, what are some of the blessings that come on believers as they obey God's Word?

_____

_____

_____

b. Deuteronomy 28:15-68

Beginning in verse 15, God categorizes the things He calls curses. In our language, what are some of the curses that come on those who do not obey God's Word?

_____

_____

_____

c. In examining Deuteronomy 28, please circle the correct answer. God categorizes,

healing and health	a blessing or a curse
sickness and disease	a blessing or a curse
prosperity and success	a blessing or a curse
poverty and lack	a blessing or a curse
disaster and tragedy	a blessing or a curse

A blessing is not a curse. A curse is not a "blessing in disguise." God's blessings are true blessings. When God calls something a curse, it is a curse! We can clearly see that healing, good health and prosperity are God's will for every believer. To be healthy and prosperous is a blessing. Health and prosperity are part of the abundant life Jesus came to bring.

E. PERSONAL APPLICATION

You may wish to study this area further. There are many good books on the subject. In addition, here are some ideas for your own biblical study in this area.

1. Study healing in the ministry of Jesus. A careful reading of the Gospels — Matthew, Mark, Luke and John — will be helpful. Remember, Jesus is the same yesterday, today and forever, according to Hebrews 13:8. Whatever we see Him doing in His earthly ministry, He is still doing today through His Body, the Church.

2. Study the prosperity of the Old Testament patriarchs. Remember, we are under a new and better covenant. What God did for people in the Old Testament, He will do for us as we walk in the light of His Word.

    a. Abraham — Genesis 12-25

    b. Isaac — Genesis 25-28

    c. Jacob — Genesis 27-49

    d. Joseph — Genesis 37-50

    e. Moses — Exodus - Deuteronomy

    f. Joshua — Joshua 1:8

F. GROUP EXERCISE

If there are those in your group who are experiencing lack, poverty, sickness or hardship, you may want to take time to pray for one another. Look at James 5:14-16.

¹James Strong, *The Exhaustive Concordance Compact Edition with Dictionaries of Hebrew and Greek Words* (Grand Rapids: Baker Book House, 1992) "Greek Dictionary of the New Testament," p. 57, #4051, #4052, #4053.

CHAPTER TWELVE

HOW TO BE AN OVERCOMER

As a new Christian, you have begun an eternal adventure to know and to walk with God. Our God is a good Father. He desires that all of His children walk in victory on the earth. He desires that we grow and develop spiritually so that we overcome the trials and tests that the world, the devil and our own flesh bring against us.

Living a victorious Christian life doesn't mean that we will never face any adversities, but it does mean that through God's help we can overcome every single one! God will always cause us to triumph as we trust Him. As Christians, Jesus has provided everything we need to walk in victory. Through His death and resurrection, He made it possible for us to walk free from all sin, sickness and poverty; however, we have an adversary who wants to rob us of this life of victory. Our enemy wants to stunt our spiritual growth and our influence on others for Christ. Satan will try to depress, oppress and afflict our spirits, minds and bodies to keep us from being effective in our walk with God and in our witness for Christ to others.

As we recognize this spiritual battle and the two opposing kingdoms, as we realize who we are in Christ and our authority over the enemy through Christ, we can truly walk in victory. It is at this point that many new Christians move either forward or backward in their relationship with God. As you study and apply these Scriptures, you can be sure to move ahead with God!

A. REMEMBER, GOD IS ON YOUR SIDE

Is it really God's will for you to walk in victory?

1. John 10:10

   What quality of life did Jesus come to bring? _____

   _____

   Describe the abundant life in your own words. _____

   _____

2. 2 Corinthians 2:14

   When does God want us to triumph? _____

   Define "always" in your own words. _____

3. 1 Corinthians 15:57

What does God give us through Jesus Christ? _____

Describe victory. _____

_____

4. Romans 8:37

Who does God say we are through Christ? _____

_____

Describe someone who is more than a conqueror.

_____

_____

5. 1 John 5:4,5

If we are born of God and believe that Jesus is the Son of God, what are we promised? __

_____

To overcome the world means what? (For help, look up 1 John 2:15,16.)

6. Psalm 34:19

Does God promise us that we will never face any difficulty? _____

What does God promise to do for us? _____

_____

7. Philippians 4:13

What does God say you can do through Christ's strength? _____

8. Romans 5:17

What are we to do in life? _____

Describe someone who reigns in life. _____

_____

9. Luke 1:37

Is there anything that is impossible with God? _____

10. Philippians 4:19

What will God do for you? _____

11. 3 John 2

What is God's will for us according to this verse? _____

_____

God desires us to be prosperous in all three areas of life — in our spirit, soul and body.

Chapter 3 discussed Jesus, our Redeemer. He redeemed us from the curse of the law which included poverty, sickness and eternal death. It is God's will for His children to walk in prosperity and to be healthy in mind and body.

Are you convinced that God's will for you is to walk in victory? It would be of great spiritual benefit for you to write these verses of Scripture on index cards and read them aloud every morning. Insert your name into each verse and as you meditate on them you will begin to see yourself the same way God already sees you. Remember, God is on your side.

B. RECOGNIZE THERE ARE TWO KINGDOMS

The Bible teaches that there are two kingdoms. These two invisible kingdoms are opposed to one another. Each kingdom has a king, as well as subjects, a governmental system and a strategy. It will help you as you learn to spiritually discern these kingdoms.

1. Colossians 1:13

What power was over you before you received Jesus as Lord? _____

2. Ephesians 2:1-3

Before you became a Christian, whose power and kingdom were you under? _____

3. John 3:3

Who can see the kingdom of God? _____

Those who are born again will not only see the kingdom of God in life after death, but they will also see the kingdom of God with the eyes of their spirit in this life.

In what ways can you identify that the eyes of your spirit have been opened to spiritual things that you were blind to previously? _____

_____

4. Romans 14:17

   What three characteristics describe the kingdom of God? _____

   _____

5. Luke 17:20,21

   The kingdom of God is not visible to our outward eyes but is located where? _____

   _____

6. John 10:10

   We can see the kings of two kingdoms described in this verse.

   Describe Jesus' will as King _____

   Describe Satan's will as king _____

   This chart can help us recognize the operation of both kingdoms.

	GOD'S KINGDOM	SATAN'S KINGDOM
Type	kingdom of Light	kingdom of darkness
King	Jesus	Satan
Residents	born-again believers	all unbelievers
Quality of life	abundance	lack
Servants	angels	demons
Atmosphere	love, peace, joy, patience, kindness, gentle, faith, self-control	hatred, fear, strife, confusion, death, doubt, unbelief, pride, jealousy, selfish ambition

For further study: John 8:12; Revelation 17:14; John 8:44; Hebrews 1:13,14; Ephesians 6:12; Galatians 5:19-23

C. REALIZE YOUR AUTHORITY OVER SATAN AND HIS KINGDOM

By now you have noticed that you have an enemy. Satan, called the devil, is the adversary of the Christian. Satan's main goal is to blind the minds of unbelievers so that they do not receive Jesus as their Lord. Once a person has confessed Jesus as his Lord, Satan's next goal is to paralyze the effectiveness of that Christian's witness by seeking to destroy his faith and causing him to doubt the validity of his own salvation, the Bible, or any facet of his faith.

Since the very beginning, Satan has been trying to become a god. When the true and only God Almighty — our Father — cast Satan out of heaven to the earth, Satan began trying to destroy God's creation — man — to get back at God. However, there was one Man Satan could not destroy through sin and that Man was Jesus Christ! Jesus totally defeated Satan and has given us the legal right to His victory through His name.

Satan and Jesus are archenemies. It is not surprising that Satan is our adversary. We need not be afraid of Satan, but we do need to be aware of his devices so that we take authority, in the name of Jesus, over any of his attacks.

1. Discern Satan and his schemes

   a. Ephesians 6:12

      Recognize that you are in an invisible wrestling match; but remember, Satan is a defeated foe. Jesus Christ, in His death, burial and resurrection, overcame and defeated Satan. The fight that the Christian is called upon to fight is the good fight of faith (1 Tim. 6:12).

      Our opponent seeks to rob us of our faith in God's Word. How is our opponent, Satan, and his kingdom, described in this verse? _____

      _____

      _____

      Who are we not wrestling against? _____

   b. 1 Peter 5:8

      What is your adversary seeking to do? _____

      _____

   c. John 10:10

      What is Satan's threefold strategy? _____

      _____

   d. 2 Corinthians 2:11

      Satan can't take advantage of us as we are _____

You can always recognize Satan at work, because his devices are identical to his character. In the following chart, match the correct verses with Satan's revealed character.

_____ John 8:44 (first part of verse)		a. thief
_____ John 10:10		b. murderer
_____ John 8:44 (second part of verse)		c. liar
_____ Revelation 12:10		d. devourer
_____ 1 Peter 5:8		e. accuser
_____ 2 Corinthians 11:14		f. oppressor
_____ Acts 10:38		g. angel of light
_____ Mark 4:15		h. faith sifter
_____ Luke 22:31		i. Word stealer

Whenever you see or experience any of these attacks, you can know that Satan is behind them because that is what he seeks to do.

As a believer, you have power over the devil through the name of Jesus, and through the Word of God you can stop every attack. Let's look at how Jesus defeated the devil and the authority Jesus has given us, as believers.

2. Understand that Jesus defeated the devil

Satan is a defeated foe. When Jesus died on the cross and rose from the dead, He totally defeated the devil.

a. 1 John 3:8

What was Jesus' main purpose in coming to earth?_____

b. Colossians 2:15

What did Jesus do to Satan and his host? _____

c. Ephesians 1:20-22

Where is Jesus seated now? _____

3. Recognize your authority over the devil

Jesus has granted you a position of authority over the devil. For example, in a secular job when you are in a position of authority you have the right to grant privileges to those who are under your authority. You can send one of your employees to represent you in a meeting or to speak for you in certain situations. You can send someone on an assignment, in your name, to act as your representative. By granting someone this right, you are giving him or her authority to act as you would act, to speak on your behalf and to represent you properly.

In a real sense, everyone your representative contacts or speaks with knows that you are the one who will be responsible for fulfilling any promises he makes. Everyone knows that your representative could not possibly fulfill the promises he or she makes in your name; but they expect you, the one in authority, to make the promises good!

In the same way, Jesus Christ is in a position of authority as the King and Lord of the universe. He has the right to grant authority to anyone He wishes. Jesus has granted authority to every believer. He has given every believer the right to use His name. Jesus has given us "the power of attorney" to use His name to defeat the devil. As we exercise our authority through God's Word and in the name of Jesus, Jesus is responsible to make His promises good.

a. Mark 16:17

   Jesus gave us authority in His name. What did He tell us to do in His name concerning the devil and demons? _____

   Who has authority to cast out devils?_____

   _____

b. Luke 10:18,19

   Jesus gave us power to overcome what? _____

   _____

c. 1 John 4:4

   God lives inside of you. What does this verse say about God inside of you and the devil in the world? _____

   _____

d. Ephesians 2:6

We saw earlier that Jesus has been raised up far above all the power of the enemy (Eph. 1:20-22). Where does this Scripture say we have been raised and seated? _____

_____

Does this mean that we are seated above all the power of the enemy in Jesus' name? __

_____

4. Be familiar with your spiritual weapons

a. James 4:7

What two things are we told to do? _____

_____

What will the devil do? _____

b. 1 Peter 5:8-10

What are we told to do? _____

_____

What will God do? (v. 10.) _____

_____

c. Matthew 4:1-11

What three words did Jesus use to resist the devil? _____

What did Jesus quote after He said "It is written"? _____

5. Know how to exercise your authority over the enemy

God has given us real weapons with which we can fight the good fight of faith and enforce the enemy's defeat in our lives. Our weapons are tested and guaranteed to overcome Satan. God has not left us helpless; He has given us weapons in order to fight the good fight of faith.

a. 2 Corinthians 10:4,5

What type of weapons do we have? _____

What do our weapons do?

_____ strongholds

_____ imaginations

_____ thoughts

We can see from this passage that much of our enemy's attack is aimed against our minds: in thoughts, imaginations and, eventually, strongholds. It is important that we spend time thinking upon God's Word and do not allow the devil any foothold in our thought life.

b. Hebrews 4:12

What is sharper than any two-edged sword? _____

_____

How can we use this against the devil? _____

_____

c. Revelation 12:11

How do we overcome and enforce Satan's defeat in our lives?_____

d. Luke 10:17

In Whose name is the devil subject to us? _____

_____

Always remember that the weapons that God has given you are mighty! Remember to quote the Word of God, claim the blood of Jesus, use the name of Jesus and speak words of faith to overcome all the wiles of the devil!

D. PERSONAL APPLICATION

Perhaps you are undergoing a spiritual attack at this time. Is there an area of your life where the enemy has been harassing you, trying to discourage you or planting seeds of doubt and fear? Jesus has provided you with the power to be victorious over the enemy.

It is God's will for you **always** to triumph in Christ. He has given you mighty spiritual weapons which will always give you the victory as you use them in faith. As one preacher expressed it, "Being a Christian does not guarantee you a life lived on flowery beds of ease, but being a Christian does give you the promise of power to overcome every test and trial."

Take a moment to look at section A of this chapter: "Remember, God Is on Your Side." Any time you face a spiritual battle, meditate upon the Scriptures which promise you victory in Christ. As you mix your faith with God's Word, you will experience the victorious Christian life.

Act on these truths and you will experience victory.

1. Draw near to God. If there is any sin in your life or anything that is displeasing to God, repent of it and tell God you intend to turn around and follow after Him.

2. Speak to the particular situation in the name of Jesus and command Satan and all of his demons to stop in their maneuvers against you.

   For example: "In the name of Jesus, I command you, Satan, and all of your demons to stop in all of your maneuvers against me in the area(s) of _____." List the specific area(s), i.e., finances, guilt, temptation, sickness, etc.

3. Look up Scriptures that relate to your situation. Begin to meditate on those verses and speak them with authority as Jesus did: "It is written...." The Word of God is your offensive sword. Use it regularly to halt and dismantle the devil's attacks.

E. GROUP EXERCISE

As a group, look at Ephesians 6:10-18 and discuss the spiritual armor that God has given us. What is it? What is its purpose? How can we put it on? Look at verse 18 and consider this:

Perhaps you, or others in the group, have been facing trials and tests and or attacks of fear from the enemy. As a group, take time to pray for one another. Use your weapons to stand against the devil.

CHAPTER THIRTEEN

HOW TO SERVE GOD

A. GOD HAS A PLAN FOR YOUR LIFE

God has a wonderful plan for your life! When you became a born-again Christian, not only were you transferred from the kingdom of darkness into the kingdom of God, but you were automatically enlisted in the army of God. You have become an ambassador for Christ. As Christians, we have the wonderful privilege and responsibility of serving God and sharing the good news of Jesus Christ with others. Not only does God want you to **be blessed**, He wants you to **be a blessing**. Not only does God want to minister **to** you, He wants to minister **through** you to others. Let's look at what the Bible teaches us about serving God.

B. ALL CHRISTIANS ARE CALLED TO BE SERVANTS

1. Matthew 20:26,27

   If we want to be great in God's kingdom, what must we do? _____

2. Matthew 9:35-38

   How did Jesus describe the multitude of people? _____

   _____

   The harvest of souls (unsaved people) is plenteous, but what is lacking? _____

   What did Jesus tell us to pray for? _____

   Are you willing to be a laborer?_____

C. ALL CHRISTIANS ARE CALLED TO BE WITNESSES FOR CHRIST

1. 2 Corinthians 5:17-21

   What ministry has God called every believer to be involved in?_____

   We are called "_____ for Christ."

   In your own words, how would you define an ambassador? _____

_____

As an ambassador for Christ with the ministry of reconciliation, what are we to tell people who do not know Jesus Christ? _____

_____

2. Mark 16:15-20 and Matthew 28:18-20

What did Jesus tell us to do? _____

_____

_____

How would you summarize the Gospel, the Good News? _____

_____

_____

GOSPEL: The Gospel of Jesus Christ is good news. Gospel means good news. The good news is that although we were slaves of sin and doomed to eternal death and subject to sickness and poverty, Jesus Christ through His death on the cross, His shed blood and His burial and resurrection has once and for all released all mankind from the bondage of sin, sickness and poverty. The good news of the Gospel is that through Jesus Christ we can be reconciled to a relationship with our loving heavenly Father.

This is called the "Great Commission." Every believer has been commissioned by Jesus to go into their *world* to tell others the good news of salvation through faith in Jesus Christ.

3. Romans 10:13-15

Who can be saved? _____

Before a person can call on the Lord, he must _____

_____

Before a person can believe in Jesus, he must _____

_____

Before a person hears about Christ, there must be a _____

Will you allow God to use you to be a preacher of the Good News? _____

4. Acts 1:8

When the Holy Spirit comes upon us (when we are baptized, or filled, with the Holy Spirit), we receive power to do what? _____

In your own words, how would you define a witness?_____

_____

_____

5. 1 Corinthians 9:19-23

Who are we to serve? (v. 19.) _____

What is Paul describing in verses 20-22? _____

_____

In order to relate to sinners and to become "all things to all men," do we need to participate in ungodly practices? _____

How do we go into all the world and befriend unbelievers, becoming all things to all men, and yet maintain a lifestyle pleasing to God — being in the world but not of the world? (John 17:16.) In your own life, how do you do this?

_____

_____

_____

6. Luke 15:1-7

Who came to hear Jesus? (vv. 1,2.)_____

Who got mad at Jesus for being with sinners? _____

_____

What was Jesus telling us about the priority of finding the "lost" in verses 4-7? _____

_____

Jesus was a great example of being in the world and not of it. He knew how to be a friend to sinners without condemning them; at the same time, He was not dragged into their sin and hypocrisy.

7. Proverbs 11:30

What does a wise person do? _____

Every believer has been given the commission to go into all the world and preach the Gospel and to make disciples of all nations. There are lost people all around us. Pray and ask God which of the unsaved people you come in contact with each day you should befriend and begin to share the good news of Jesus Christ with.

In addition to being witnesses for Christ, we need to recognize that God has a unique plan and place for us in His great plan. There is nothing like finding and fulfilling the purpose for which you were created. Let's look at what the Bible says about God's will for our lives.

D. ALL CHRISTIANS SHOULD SEEK GOD'S PLAN AND WILL FOR THEIR LIVES

1. Matthew 6:33

   In our life what are we to seek first? _____

   _____

2. 1 John 2:15-17

   What are we told we should not love? _____

   _____

   What is going to happen to the world? (v. 17.)

   _____

   What will happen to the person who does God's will? _____

3. 2 Corinthians 4:18

   We can live life from a temporal perspective or an eternal perspective.

   Things that are seen are_____

   Things that are not seen are _____

   Are you spending your life and investing your time and energies in temporal or in eternal things? _____

   What changes could you make? _____

   _____

4. Mark 8:34-38

If we try to save our life and do our own thing, what will happen? (vv. 35,36.)_____

_____

If we lose our life for Jesus and the sake of the Gospel, what will happen? _____

_____

What do you think it means to "lose your life" for Jesus and the sake of the Gospel? ____

_____

This is an area where you need to use wisdom. Some young Christians, in their zeal and because of a lack of knowledge of God's Word, have foolishly *left all* for the Gospel. Some have quit their jobs, left their families, not paid their bills, gone into the streets and preached hellfire and brimstone, while running from their responsibilities as a citizen, as a husband or wife, as a parent and as an employee. Oftentimes these types of people become a menace and a burden to society, and their bad reputation affects the Body of Christ. When they left all, they left their common sense as well. This is not God's plan. This type of lifestyle does not glorify God.

The important thing, as a new or young Christian, is to have a heart attitude that says, "Lord, I give You my life. I will do what You want me to do. I will go where You want me to go. I will say what You want me to say." It may be that the Lord will have you do just exactly what you are already doing, except now you will be doing it to glorify Him.

On the other hand, God does call some people to leave their current vocation and status in life in order to serve Him in a full-time vocation. Often this type of call will include some type of formal ministerial training or an apprenticeship under a seasoned minister of the Gospel. God is not in the business of raising up "flash in the pan" superstar ministers. The type of people God uses are likely to experience years of developing a history with God. Over time, when God counts an individual faithful, He will put them in the ministry. If you sense the call of God on your life, it is wise to speak with your pastor, or an older, mature Christian who knows you. God's timing and His wisdom are important ingredients when it comes to these matters.

E. ALL CHRISTIANS SHOULD BE GOOD STEWARDS

God has given each of us the responsibility of being good stewards of all that He has given us. This includes our time, talents and our tithe (the tithe is ten percent of our income). Let's look at the subject of being good stewards.

1. Matthew 25:14-29

   In this passage we see Jesus expects a return on the talents He has given us.

   What did the Lord say about those who were good stewards of their talents? (vv. 20-23.)

   _____

   What did the Lord say to the servant who was a bad steward of his talent? (vv. 24-29.) __

   _____

2. 1 Peter 4:10

   Who has received gifts?_____

   What are we to do with the gifts we have received? _____

   Perhaps you wonder what specific things God has given you stewardship over. What gifts and talents has He given you? Each of us is to be a good steward with our time, tithe and talents. To get started in identifying and being a good steward of your time, talents and tithe, ask yourself these simple questions:

   How do I spend my time?

   What gifts, talents or abilities do I think God has given me?

   What type of things do I enjoy doing?

   What type of things am I good at doing?

   What talents have other people recognized in me?

   What are the needs around me that would benefit from my talents?

   Can I glorify God with my talents and gifts?

   How do I spend my money?

   What percentage of my finances do I give to advancing the Gospel and helping others?

F. DEDICATED AND CONSECRATED TO THE WILL OF GOD

As you have studied this chapter on serving God, maybe you have been challenged to give your life completely to the Lord. There is nothing like being totally consecrated to God's plan for your life. There is no freedom like the freedom of totally surrendering to God's will. If you have never given Jesus Christ the complete lordship over your life and your future, saying a prayer like the one that follows, from your heart, can be your first step toward serving God effectively.

> Dear Father God, I come before You in the name of Jesus. I give myself completely to You and to Your will for my life. Lord Jesus, when I see You, I want to hear You say, "Well done, good and faithful servant," so I surrender and yield to You. Have Your way in and through me. Holy Spirit, help me to be a bold witness for Jesus Christ. Help me to stand perfect and complete in all Your will, Lord. Help me to be a good steward of my time, talents and tithe. I will go where You want me to go. I will do what You want me to do. I will say what You want me to say. I dedicate and consecrate myself to You, Lord, in Jesus' name. Amen.

G. PERSONAL APPLICATION

Lifestyle evangelism and disciple-making should be the goal of every Christian. That is, our very lifestyle should be one of leading others to Jesus Christ and establishing them in the basic truths of God's Word. Consider this faith-adventure challenge:

1. Pray and ask God for one or more persons with whom you can share the good news of Jesus Christ. Make a list of your non-believing friends.

2. Pray and ask God for one or more new, or young, Christians that you can help to establish in the basic truths of God's Word. Make a list of your new, or young, Christian friends.

3. Invite these individuals to join you in a thirteen-week study through this workbook. Ask them to commit to a specific time, day and place, once a week for thirteen weeks.

4. Pray and trust God to use you! Teach them what you've learned from God's Word and this workbook.

H. GROUP EXERCISE

Challenge each person in the group to become a committed and vital part of a local, Bible-based, Word-oriented church. Encourage each person to get involved serving God by doing the following:

1. **Commit yourself.** Offer your heart, time, talents and tithe to a local church. Get behind a pastor and a church vision you can believe in. One of the best things to do is let your pastor know that you are committed and available. Pastors cannot read minds. Oftentimes, unless you tell him, he does not know that you are committed and available to serve. Once you have committed yourself, trust God to give your pastor wisdom on where you can start serving.

2. **Humble yourself.** Once you commit yourself to be involved in a local church, take the necessary steps to get involved. Many churches have specific steps that you must follow if you want to serve in that church. Do whatever it takes to be involved. If it means taking a membership class, other foundations classes, or even more, do it. In some churches, this process may take as long as one year, or more. Your attitude during this time of orientation and preparation is important. Keep a humble heart.

3. **Be teachable.** Take advantage of every opportunity for training, growth and spiritual development that the church offers. Never become a "know it all." Stay teachable and you will continue to grow.

4. **Start serving.** Every pastor is looking for faithful people who are willing to do anything that needs to be done. Be faithful in little things. Be on time. Complete your tasks. Keep a good attitude. Work with excellence. Trust God to promote you to the areas where your gifts will best be utilized. The Bible tells us that a man's gift will make a way for him. (Prov. 18:16.) Don't force your way into positions of service. Maintain a servant's heart and God will open the doors He has for you.

CONCLUSION

Congratulations on your new life in Christ. You have begun an exciting, supernatural relationship with God. As you follow Him, with your whole heart, He will bless you greatly and use you to introduce others to Jesus Christ. May God bless you with a fruitful life to His glory.

If this workbook has been meaningful to you, please introduce others to the contents within. May we challenge you to lead others into the knowledge of God through *Getting a Grip on the Basics*, which presents truths that every Christian needs for building a firm foundation for the victorious Christian life.

HOW TO RECOGNIZE FALSE DOCTRINES

Look at Ephesians 4:14,15. We are instructed to grow up spiritually, so that we will not be tossed to and fro with every wind of doctrine. There are many voices and doctrines clamoring for our attention. It is important to be established in the truth, so you can easily recognize what is false. Do you know how to recognize a counterfeit dollar bill? Become so familiar with the real dollar bill that when you see a counterfeit you will know it, instantly. In the same way, as we become so familiar with the true Bible doctrines, we can, instantly, recognize the false doctrines that blow our way.

There are many cults, false religions, humanistic teachings and occult groups who promote doctrines clearly opposed to what is revealed in the Bible. The best rule of thumb is to ask, "Can these teachings be supported by Scripture? Is there anything in the Bible that would contradict these teachings?" Some groups will use just enough Scripture to sound biblical. The Bible tells us that by the testimony of two or three witnesses let everything be established. (2 Cor. 13:1.) It is important to find two or three, or more, verses of Scripture...**in their context**...that support a particular doctrine. If someone teaches something based upon one verse taken out of context, this is a good sign that the doctrine is false.

Detailed below are some of the foundational, true doctrines that false teachers will negate, twist or use to deceive.

1. **The deity of Christ: Jesus Christ is actually God in the flesh, the second person of the Trinity.**

   (John 5:18; John 10:30-33; John 20:28; Col. 1:15-19.)

   False teachers will deny the deity of Christ. They will call Jesus a great moral teacher, a prophet or just a good man, but they will deny that He was God in the flesh.

2. **The Virgin Birth of Christ: Mary was a virgin, and she was "with child" by the Holy Spirit.**

   (Isa. 7:14; Matt. 1:18-23; Luke 1:30-35.)

   False teachers will deny the Virgin Birth of Christ. They will take an intellectual, scientific approach and deny the miracle of a virgin being with child.

3. **The Bible is the inspired Word of God. The Scriptures are infallible and inerrant.**

   (2 Tim. 3:16; Heb. 4:12; 2 Peter 1:19-21.)

   False teachers will deny the inspiration of the Word of God. They will attempt to discredit the veracity of God's Word and reduce its authority as God's Word to man.

4. The blood of Jesus was shed for the remission of our sins.

(Matt. 26:27,28; Col. 1:14; Heb. 9:12-14,22.)

False teachers will deny the importance of the blood of Jesus. They will attempt to negate sin, man's guilt, and, therefore, the need for the spotless blood of the Lamb of God for the remission of sin.

5. The death, burial and resurrection of Christ was substitutional and valid.

(John 20:1-9; Acts 1:1-3; 1 Cor. 15:12-17.)

False teachers will usually agree that a man named Jesus died on a cross and was buried; however, when it comes to the resurrection of Christ, they will deny it as a historical fact. The resurrection is the crux of a Christian's faith. The resurrection of Christ is the fundamental truth that the early church preached. To deny the resurrection is to void the Christian's hope of eternal life after the grave. As Paul said, **And if Christ be not raised, your faith is vain; ye are yet in your sins** (1 Cor. 15:17).

6. The Godhead is made up of the Trinity — Father, Son and Holy Spirit.

(Matt. 28:19; 2 Cor. 13:14; 1 John 5:7.)

False teachers will deny the existence of the Trinity. If they do acknowledge the three persons — Father, Son and Holy Spirit — they will not call them co-equal. In fact, they will accuse Christians of teaching polytheism: the plurality of gods. As Christians, we believe that there is one God Who consists of three persons: the Father, Son and Holy Spirit.

7. After Creation, man fell; salvation was made available through repentance and the shed blood of Christ. Salvation is received by faith through grace to whosoever will believe on Jesus Christ.

(John 3:16; John 14:6; Rom. 6:23; Eph. 2:8,9.)

False teachers will deny the need for repentance, or faith for salvation. Often they will promote such doctrines as salvation by good works (the idea that we can work through our efforts and good works to obtain salvation); universal salvation (the idea that everyone will be saved in the end — including Satan, himself); relativism (the idea that you can believe anything you want to believe about God and salvation. They deny Jesus as the way, truth and life, and consider Him to be one of many ways to God. There are no absolutes, everything is relative); or even reincarnation (the idea that we go on to another plane, or form of life, in our next life).

8. The return of Jesus Christ is imminent.

(Matt. 24:1-51; Acts 1:9-11; 1 Thess. 4:15-17.)

False teachers will not only deny the resurrection, but they will deny the physical, bodily return of the Lord Jesus Christ as an event that will actually take place.

9. There is a literal heaven and a literal hell.

(Matt. 25:31-46; Luke 16:19-26; Rev. 21:1-8.)

False teachers will deny the existence of either heaven or hell, or both. Most often, their claim is that "a loving God could never send anyone to hell." The Bible teaches that there is a real hell and a real heaven. God doesn't send people to hell; but, because of their own choice to reject Jesus Christ as Lord, they send themselves to hell.

10. There is a final judgment — one for unbelievers and one for believers.

(John 12:47,48; 2 Cor. 5:10; Rev. 20:12-15.)

False teachers will deny the reality of the final judgment. The Bible teaches that we are appointed once to die, and then the judgment. (Heb. 9:27.) *Unbelievers* will stand at the Great White Throne Judgment because they have not believed on or received Jesus Christ, their names are not written in the Lamb's Book of Life and they will have to face an eternal death in hell in the lake of fire. (Rev. 20:11-15.) *Believers* will stand at the Judgment Seat of Christ (Rom. 14:10) where our works as believers will be judged and rewarded. (1 Cor. 3:10-15.)

Learn these foundational truths. Study these subjects, in depth, using your own Bible. As you become familiar with the truth, it will be easy for you to recognize things which are false.

Also, be alert when you notice the following types of things:

An exclusive attitude — the idea that this group, or teacher, is the only group with the truth.

Leaders, or teachers, who court your allegiance to them, personally. We follow Jesus, not other men or women.

Books or "revelations" that people introduce that are contradictory to the Bible. The Bible is the final standard and authority. We do not accept anything that contradicts the written Word of God.

Trust your "gut" feeling when you sense something, or someone, is teaching false doctrine. The Holy Spirit, living within you, will alert you to false doctrines if you will follow your spirit. If you suspect that you have encountered false doctrines or teachings, but you are not certain, talk to your pastor or other Christian leaders whom you trust.

HOW TO FIND A GOOD CHURCH

As a new, or young, Christian it is important to find a good church. If church life was meaningless to you in the past, or is a foreign environment to you, you may wonder why finding a good church is so important. You may wonder what you should look for in a church. You may wonder what to do when you find a good church. Before we look at these areas, there is one golden rule that you must bear in mind at all times.

The Golden Rule in How To Find a Good Church: **Realize that the perfect church does not exist!**

If you are looking for the perfect church, then you might as well stop now. Churches are made up of imperfect people with a desire to serve and follow a perfect God. God is perfect, churches are not. Besides, as one preacher said, "If you ever found the perfect church, you would ruin it the first day you attended!" With that in mind, here are some helpful hints on finding a good church.

REASONS TO FIND A GOOD CHURCH

Read Acts 2:41,42. From these verses, we can see four great reasons the first church gathered together; those reasons are valid for us today.

1. You need good doctrine.

The best and healthiest way to grow, as a Christian, is to feed on good doctrine. There is plenty of bad doctrine in the world and among false religions. You want to start your Christian life by being instructed and established in good Bible-based doctrine. Doctrine, which consists of the basic fundamental beliefs, is to a Christian what a solid foundation is to a building. With the proper foundation, the rest of the building will go up properly and will be secure. In the same way, with proper doctrine as our foundation, a Christian will grow up strong and healthy.

A good church will have a pastor, and possibly other leaders, who are gifted by God to teach the Word. These people are responsible to teach sound, biblical doctrine, just as the apostles did in the early church. Look for a church that teaches basic things such as: salvation by faith in the shed blood of Jesus Christ; the Bible as the inspired Word of God; the Trinity as the three persons of the Godhead — Father, Son and Holy Spirit; the baptism in the Spirit; the importance of evangelism and discipleship; the goodness of God demonstrated by healing, the abundant life and the walk of victory in Christ. You will want to find a church where there is a spirit of faith, not an attitude of doom and condemnation.

2. You need fellowship.

God didn't create you to be a "lone ranger." He created you with a need, and a desire, for friendships of various levels. As a Christian, you need the other members of the Body of

Christ for encouragement and fellowship. Sometimes we need spiritual fellowship, and at other times, we just need Christian friends with whom we can enjoy wholesome fun.

A good church ought to be like a family. When you were born again you became a member of God's family. He wants you to be involved with other members of the family of God. When you become a Christian, your natural family and friends don't always understand your life. A good church family will be there to support and encourage you in the Lord.

3. You need the breaking of bread.

You might wonder what this means. In the early church, the term "breaking of bread" became the name for the institution of the Lord's Supper. It is during this ordinance of the church that we remember what the broken body and shed blood of Jesus means to us. We can thank Him for the healing which He provided for us through His broken body and for the forgiveness of our sin which He provided for us through His shed blood.

A good church will celebrate the Lord's Supper on a regular basis.

4. You need prayer.

Faith-filled, Spirit-led prayer is one of the mightiest tools God has given us. As we yield ourselves to God's Spirit in prayer, we can find and follow His plan and purpose for our lives, our families, our church and our community. Prayer is our vital link to heaven and God's resources. A good church will place an emphasis on prayer. It is important to find a praying church: a church that teaches you how to pray and sets aside time for prayer.

WHAT TO LOOK FOR IN A GOOD CHURCH

Read Ephesians 4:11-16. This passage of Scripture teaches us some of the things that will be found in a good church.

1. Look for a church with a strong pastor.

One of the gifts that God gives to the Body of Christ is pastors. It is important to find a church with a strong pastor. A strong pastor is someone who has a definite call from God to be a pastor. A strong pastor will have a loving and caring heart like Jesus did when He looked upon the multitudes and saw that they were like a sheep without a shepherd. A strong pastor will be a servant; his or her attitude will not be that of a dictator, but that of a servant. A strong pastor will be a leader with a vision for fulfilling what God has called his church to do. A strong pastor will teach and preach the Bible, not man's ideas, traditions or doctrines.

Generally speaking, churches that are run by boards, committees, elders or small, controlling groups tend to have problems really moving ahead with God's plan. They tend to get bogged down in meetings, bureaucracy and politics. It seems to be God's best plan to have a church that is led by a strong pastor who is surrounded by those who can provide godly counsel and wisdom when called upon.

2. Look for a church that teaches and perfects the believers for the work of the ministry.

As a believer it is important to be a part of a church that is helping you to do the work of the ministry. By "work of the ministry" we mean anything that has to do with building up the Body of Christ. This includes the ministry of reconciliation (soulwinning) that every believer has been entrusted with, as well as other areas of helps ministries, teaching and preaching. A good church will be teaching and equipping you so that you can function in the place that God has designed for you.

3. Look for a church that teaches and challenges you to grow up spiritually.

As a new Christian, you are a "babe in Christ," but you don't want to remain a spiritual baby. Over time, and with the proper instruction, you should begin to grow spiritually. It is heartbreaking to see a person who has been a Christian for a good many years but who is still a baby, spiritually speaking. A good church will speak the truth in love and challenge you to grow. At times you will need loving correction, gentle instruction and occasional reproof to help you grow into mature spiritual adulthood. A good church will challenge you to develop your own personal relationship with God through Jesus Christ. This type of church will help make you a disciple of Christ, so you are developing a healthy dependence upon the Lord and His Word. A good church will provide anything necessary to teach and challenge you to grow up into Him.

4. Look for a church with a loving atmosphere.

There is just something about feeling "at home" in church. One of the joys of the Christian life is to be a part of a church family that loves and cares for one another. This is the type of church that edifies itself in love.

A loving church family, led by a loving pastor, will be there when needs arise in your life. Perhaps there will be a time when you will need someone to perform a marriage, a funeral, water baptism, a baby dedication, hospital visitations or pray for you or those in your family who are sick. Perhaps you will need food, clothing or material things, at some time. When you are an active part of a local church, that church family will be there to help meet your needs. A church with an atmosphere of love, forgiveness and acceptance is the type of church in which you will grow and blossom.

WHAT TO DO WHEN YOU FIND A GOOD CHURCH

Read Matthew 6:33 and 1 Corinthians 6:19,20. In these Scriptures, we can see that we are to seek first God's kingdom. We can also see that we are not our own, but we belong to God. We are told to live our lives in such a way as to glorify God. One of the best ways to seek first God's kingdom and to glorify God is to be involved in helping to fulfill the vision God has given to your pastor. How can you seek God's kingdom and glorify God through a local church? Two words can sum it up: BE FAITHFUL.

1. Be faithful with your time.

First, be faithful to attend church on a regular basis. The only way you can get to know the heartbeat of a church is to attend regularly. That doesn't mean you have to be there every time the doors are open, but determine to regularly attend Sunday mornings and/or Sunday night and/or the midweek service. If you are in the process of finding a church home, then visit a church for at least a month to get an accurate picture of what the church is all about. Make a point to get to know some of the people. Ask church leaders the questions that are important to you. Make the most of your time by attending a variety of things the church has to offer.

2. Be faithful with your attitude.

Be teachable. Don't be a know-it-all. Be open to hear and receive God's Word. Avoid being critical. Do what the Bible says and walk in love — believing the best about everyone, including the pastor and the church leaders. Don't be offended if everyone doesn't reach out to you like you expect. You take the initiative to meet people, to find out what types of programs, classes and activities the church offers. Be free from unrealistic expectations. Don't be a complainer or a murmurer. Don't have an attitude that says, "Well, if I were the pastor...I would do this...I wouldn't do that...I can't believe they are going to do this." Church leaders and church members are just ordinary people who are doing their best to follow and obey God. Be merciful and supportive in your attitudes. One negative spark can light a whole church on fire. If you can't say something nice or edifying to others in the church, about the church, then don't say anything at all. If you find that you don't understand things that are happening in the church, then make it a point to talk directly to the pastor or those in leadership. Avoid being a negative person in your speech or in your attitudes.

3. Be faithful with your talents.

The best way to feel a part of a church, to meet other people and to grow with a church family is to get involved. Use your talents and do something. Find out where and how you can get involved in the church. If there are church-worker classes to take, then sign up. Let the pastor, or those in leadership, know that you desire and are willing to get involved wherever they need your help. You would be amazed at how significant your contribution to the church can be. Perhaps you are gifted to work with children, or maybe you have a bubbly, outgoing personality or great organizational skills. Be faithful to make your talents available. Don't be discouraged if you aren't asked to do the very specific thing you wanted to do. Sometimes you need to prove yourself faithful in little things before you can be entrusted to do other things. Trust the pastor and the church leaders to use you where the needs are the greatest. In due season, as the Bible teaches, when God has counted you faithful, He will put you in the ministry that your heart desires, the ministry that He has given you the talents to fulfill.

4. Be faithful in your commitments.

Be a person of your word. If you say that you will be somewhere, then be sure to follow through. If you say that you will be involved in a particular part of the church, then be faithful to the end of your commitment. Don't quit halfway through. Be faithful to prepare and fulfill your commitments. Do everything with a spirit of excellence. Avoid the "this is good enough to get by" mentality. God's kingdom and the work of God deserve nothing less than excellence. Pay attention to details and avoid being sloppy in your commitments. Be the kind of person who can be counted upon. Be the kind of person that exemplifies commitment!

5. Be faithful with your resources.

Be faithful to use your resources to further the Gospel through your church. If God has enabled you to prosper in financial and material things, be generous in your giving. Remember, God has given you the ability to obtain wealth so that He may establish His covenant on the earth. (Deut. 8:18.) He certainly wants you as a believer to be blessed in life and to enjoy abundance, but be sure to keep a healthy perspective on cheerful and generous giving. The Bible teaches that the tithe, which is ten percent of your increase, or income, belongs to the Lord and should be brought to the storehouse, the local church that you attend. In addition, we are commanded by God to give offerings to worthy ministries that are propagating the gospel of the Lord Jesus Christ and to give alms to those who are poor and in need of material things.

It is sad to say that many Christians will trust God in other areas of their lives, but when it comes to money, they keep a tight grip on their wallets. Don't have a stingy spirit. Be known as a giver. Be faithful with your material and financial resources by giving to your local church. Make a decision to be a regular, committed tither and offering and alms giver. Be a faithful channel God can flow through in the area of giving. Trust God to multiply your giving back to you, so you will have more to give!

About The Author

Beth Jones is a Bible teacher, author, wife and mother of four children, who ministers the Word in a relevant, humorous and inspiring way by sharing down-to-earth insights. She is the author of the popular Getting A Grip on the Basics series, which is being used by thousands of churches in America and abroad. She's also written the Bite-Sized Bible Study series and The Question Series of mini books. Beth writes the free, daily Jump Start eDevo for over 5000 subscribers and hosts the bethjones.org website. She and her husband, Jeff, founded and serve as the senior pastors of the growing congregation at Valley Family Church in Kalamazoo, Michigan.

Beth can be reached @ **www.bethjones.org**

Beth Jones Ministries
2500 Vincent Avenue
Kalamazoo, Michigan 49024
269-324-5599

Prayer of Salvation

God loves you--no matter who you are, no matter what your past. God loves you so much that He gave His one and only begotten Son for you. The Bible tells us that "…whoever believes in him shall not perish but have eternal life" (John 3:16 NIV). Jesus laid down His life and rose again so that we could spend eternity with Him in heaven and experience His absolute best on earth. If you would like to receive Jesus into your life, say the following prayer out loud and mean it from your heart.

Heavenly Father, I come to You admitting that I am a sinner. Right now, I choose to turn away from sin, and I ask You to cleanse me of all unrighteousness. I believe that Your Son, Jesus, died on the cross to take away my sins. I also believe that He rose again from the dead so that I might be forgiven of my sins and made righteous through faith in Him. I call upon the name of Jesus Christ to be the Savior and Lord of my life. Jesus, I choose to follow You and ask that You fill me with the power of the Holy Spirit. I declare that right now I am a child of God. I am free from sin and full of the righteousness of God. I am saved in Jesus' name. Amen.

If you prayed this prayer to receive Jesus Christ as your Savior for the first time, please contact us on the web at www.harrisonhouse.com to receive a free book.

Or you may write to us at
Harrison House
P.O. Box 35035
Tulsa, Oklahoma 74153

THE HARRISON HOUSE VISION

Proclaiming the truth and the power

Of the Gospel of Jesus Christ

With excellence;

Challenging Christians to

Live victoriously,

Grow spiritually,

Know God intimately.

Bible Studies By Beth Jones

GRIP SERIES

Getting A Grip On The Basics For Kids

Getting A Grip On The Basics For Teens

Getting A Grip On Serving God

Getting A Grip On Health And Healing

Getting A Grip On Prosperous Living

Afirmandose En Los Principios Basicos

BITE SIZED SERIES

Satisfied Lives For Desperate Housewives
God's Word On Proverbs 31
Great Study For Women, Retail $12.99
ISBN: 1-933433-04-3

Session 1: Desperate For God
Session 2: Desperate For Balance
Session 3: Desperate For A Good Marriage
Session 4: Desperate For Godly Kids
Session 5: Desperate To Serve
Session 6: Desperate For Purpose

Grace For The Pace
God's Word For Stressed & Overloaded Lives
Great Study For Men & Women, Retail $7.99
ISBN: 1-933433-02-7
Session 1: Escape From Hamsterville

Session 2: Help Is Here
Session 3: How Do You Spell Relief?
Session 4: Get A Bigger Frying Pan
Session 5: Houston, We Have A Problem!
Session 6: Time Keeps On Ticking

Kissed Or Dissed
God's Word For Feeling Rejected & Overlooked
Great Study For Women, Retail $7.99
ISBN: 1-933433-01-9
Session 1: Dissed 101

Session 2: Blessed & Highly Favored
Session 3: Edit Your Life
Session 4: That's What I'm Talking About
Session 5: Sow Acceptance Seeds
Session 6: Just Like Jesus

What To Do When You Feel Blue
God's Word For Depression & Discouragement
Great Study For Men & Women, Retail $7.99
ISBN: 1-933433-00-0

Session 1: When The Sky Is Not Blue
Session 2: No Pity Parties Allowed
Session 3: The Things You Could Think
Session 4: Go To Your Happy Place
Session 5: You've Got To Have Friends
Session 6: Lift Up The Down

The Friends God Sends
God's Word On Friendship & Chick Chat
Great Study For Women, Retail $7.99
ISBN: 1-933433-05-1
Session 1: Friendship Realities

Session 2: The Friendship Workout
Session 3: God-Knit Friendships
Session 4: Who's On Your Boat?
Session 5: Anatomy of A Friendship Famine
Session 6: A Friend of God

Don't Factor Fear Here
God's Word For Overcoming Anxiety, Fear & Phobias
Great Study For Men & Women, Retail $12.99
ISBN: 1-933433-03-5
Session 1: Fear of Death

Session 2: Fear of Man
Session 3: Fear of Danger
Session 4: Fear of Change
Session 5: Fear Factors - Peace & Love
Session 6: Fear Factors - Faith & Courage

Call Or Go Online To Order:
800-596-0379 www.bethjones.org

visit Beth online...

FREE

Subscribe
to
Beth's
Daily Devotionals

Jump Start
Daily E-Devo